DBT
WORKBOOK
—— FOR ——
ADULTS

How to Use Dialectical Behavior Therapy Skills for Easy Anxiety Management, Relationship Success, Emotion Regulation, and Trauma Recovery

ANNA NIERLING

© Copyright 2023 - All rights reserved.

The content contained within this book may not be reproduced, duplicated or transmitted without direct written permission from the author or the publisher.

Under no circumstances will any blame or legal responsibility be held against the publisher, or author, for any damages, reparation, or monetary loss due to the information contained within this book, either directly or indirectly.

Legal Notice:

This book is copyright protected. It is only for personal use. You cannot amend, distribute, sell, use, quote or paraphrase any part, or the content within this book, without the consent of the author or publisher.

Disclaimer Notice:

Please note the information contained within this document is for educational and entertainment purposes only. All effort has been executed to present accurate, up to date, reliable, complete information. No warranties of any kind are declared or implied. Readers acknowledge that the author is not engaged in the rendering of legal, financial, medical or professional advice. The content within this book has been derived from various sources. Please consult a licensed professional before attempting any techniques outlined in this book.

By reading this document, the reader agrees that under no circumstances is the author responsible for any losses, direct or indirect, that are incurred as a result of the use of the information contained within this document, including, but not limited to, errors, omissions, or inaccuracies.

CONTENTS

INTRODUCTION: Discovering Your Path to Inner Peace with Dialectical Behavior Therapy   1
    Why DBT Is Meaningful to Me   4

CHAPTER 1: Week One — Strengthening DBT with Present Moment Awareness   7
    The Power of Mindfulness: What Skills   11
    Describing   13
    Participate   15
    Practical Exercises   16
    The Power of Mindfulness: The 'How' Skills   18
    Non-Judgmentally: Free Yourself from Criticism   20
    Key Takeaways for Week 1   22

CHAPTER 2: Week Two — Finding Balance and Mindfulness   25
    My Mom and Mindfulness   27
    Key Takeaways for Week 2   37

CHAPTER 3: Week Three — Distress Tolerance   39
    What is Distress Tolerance?   39
    Distress Tolerance and Acceptance   41
    TIPP Skills: Your Fast-Acting Rescue   42
    Key Takeaways for Week 3   56

CHAPTER 4: Week 4— Radical Acceptance   59
    Understanding Radical Acceptance   59
    The Roots of Radical Acceptance: DBT   62
    Key Takeaways Week 4   71

CHAPTER 5: Week 5 — Emotional Regulation — 73

    What is Emotion Regulation? — 74
    The Three Thinking Styles — 74
    Chain Analysis Exercises — 77
    Primary vs. Secondary Emotions — 83
    Key Takeaways Week 5 — 87

CHAPTER 6: Week 6 — Emotional Regulation Toolbox — 89

    Using ABC PLEASE to Manage Your Emotions — 90
    How to Use Opposite Actions — 95
    Problem Solving — 101
    Five Options For Solving Any Problem — 104
    Key Takeaways Week 6 — 107

CHAPTER 7: Week 7 — Interpersonal Effectiveness — 111

    What Is Interpersonal Effectiveness? — 112
    What Is Emotional Effectiveness? — 113
    Clarifying Your Priorities — 115
    Levels of Intensity — 117
    DEAR MAN — 118
    DEAR MAN Exercise: Making a Plan — 120
    Key Takeaways Week 7 — 123

CHAPTER 8: Understanding the Power of Validation — 125

    The Six Levels of Validation — 125
    GIVE Skills — 130
    Morgan's Story — 132
    FAST Skills — 134
    Combining the Skills — 138
    Key Takeaways Week 8 — 140

CONCLUSION — 143

CONTINUING THE JOURNEY — 143

REFERENCES — 147

INTRODUCTION

Discovering Your Path to Inner Peace with Dialectical Behavior Therapy

Welcome to a place of healing, support, and personal well-being.

I get it- starting on the path to feeling better can feel pretty overwhelming. I'm here to offer you guidance with care and understanding.

As we go through this workbook together, we'll take things one step at a time. My main goal is to assist you in feeling better as well as equip you with the tools and support you need to handle life's challenges. I also aim to nurture a sense of peace and well-being throughout your journey.

I know that seeking help can sometimes feel awkward, uncomfortable, and even scary, but please know that you're not alone in this. I'm here to create a safe and comforting space where you can explore your emotions, deal with tricky situations, and ultimately find the healing you absolutely deserve.

I understand that life can sometimes feel like an endless exhausting loop, with emotions that seem to have a mind of their own. Perhaps you've faced moments when your thoughts race uncontrollably, your emotions overwhelm you, and your relationships feel like a tangled web of confusion. Trust me, I've been there too.

Let me share my own story with you. My journey into the world of mental health disorders began with learning about my mom. Initially diagnosed with Bipolar Disorder, her true diagnosis turned out to be Borderline Personality Disorder.

I wasn't even 8 years old when I began to realize that my mother was different. On one particular day, she took me and my older brother to the local park to play. It should have been a day of laughter and fun, but it took an unexpected turn.

"Why are there so many people here?" she wondered aloud.

"We should have come earlier," she grumbled

"Can you see them staring at us?" she anxiously asked.

"You know what? I want to go home now," she pressed.

It wasn't the first time I had witnessed my mother's mood swings, but this time was different. I started noticing that the other mothers weren't as emotionally unpredictable as mine. It was the beginning of my travels into understanding BPD without even knowing what it was yet.

Describing BPD, psychologist Marsha Linehan aptly wrote, "People with BPD are like people with third-degree burns over 90% of their bodies. Lacking emotional skin, they feel agony at the slightest touch or movement" (Goodreads, n.d.).

For those diagnosed with BPD, the world around them often feels overwhelming. Noises can become unbearable, intimacy can feel suffocating, and people can be emotionally exhausting. BPD sufferers may even believe that their own personalities are too much, fearing that their emotional volatility makes them hard to love. My mother would shower us with passionate love one moment, only to withdraw and become emotionally distant the next.

My mother's initial diagnosis was Bipolar Disorder Type 2. The symptoms were misunderstood, and she fell into the 40% of patients who meet BPD criteria but are initially misdiagnosed with Bipolar Disorder (Ruggero et al., 2010). It's easy to see why, as the symptoms often overlap and both can include mood swings, impulsive behaviors, and suicidal thoughts. However, BPD's unique aspects, such as shame, fear of abandonment, and chronic feelings of emptiness, couldn't be properly addressed by bipolar disorder treatment.

It wasn't until I turned 20 that my mother received the correct diagnosis. I could sense her relief when a doctor told her that she wasn't crazy and that her condition wasn't something to be ashamed of. "We are all complicated," the doctor said, "and you can learn to live with your complexities."

Decades have passed since my mother began accepting her BPD diagnosis and embracing those complexities. Growing up with the highs and lows of being raised by a mentally ill mother inspired me to pursue a degree in psychology and dedicate my life to supporting, helping and understanding the uniqueness of the mind.

What is my hope for you? By the time you've finished this workbook, you'll have a toolbox filled with powerful skills to:

- **Regulate your emotions.** Say 'goodbye' to feeling overwhelmed by anger, sadness, or anxiety. You'll learn how to manage and control your emotions effectively.
- **Improve your relationships.** Say 'hello' to healthier interactions with your loved ones. DBT will equip you with the tools to communicate and connect more effectively.

- **Boost your mental resilience.** Say 'farewell' to the constant barrage of negative thoughts. You'll develop the ability to calm your mind and find peace within yourself.
- **Enhance your quality of life.** Say 'yes' to living a life that aligns with your values, free from the constraints of impulsive behaviors and emotional chaos.

Why DBT Is Meaningful to Me

You might be wondering, "*Why should I trust this author?*" Well, you're absolutely right to ask. Here's the scoop: I'm not just an armchair expert on DBT. I've dedicated my life to understanding and applying these principles because of my personal experiences growing up with a mom with BPD, as well as my academic background in psychology. I've seen DBT work wonders both in my life and in my mom's, and in the lives of countless others. So, consider me your friendly guide on this journey.

How to Use This Self-Directed Workbook

Now, you might be aware that traditional DBT therapy involves various modes of treatment, including group skills training, individual therapy, phone skills coaching, and therapist consultation teams. While these modes are invaluable, this workbook is designed for the self-directed learner.

But here's the good news: DBT skills and exercises are incredibly useful on their own, even without the full complement of treatment modes. Think of this workbook as your personal DBT coach, always at your side, ready to assist you.

Before we dive into the practical exercises and transformative knowledge, let's make sure we're on the same page about what DBT is all about:

- **Marsha Linehan and the balance between acceptance and change.** DBT was developed by Marsha Linehan, a pioneer in the field of psychology. Her approach strikes a delicate balance between accepting where you are right now and empowering you to make positive changes in your life (Emeritus, 2019).
- **DBT as an adaptation of CBT.** DBT is an adaptation of Cognitive Behavioral Therapy (CBT), tailored specifically to address emotional dysregulation, self-destructive behaviors, and interpersonal challenges.
- **The four core principles.** DBT rests on four foundational principles: Mindfulness, Distress Tolerance, Emotion Regulation, and Interpersonal Effectiveness. These principles are your compass for navigating the challenges of life.

As we journey through this workbook, you'll become intimately familiar with these core principles and how to apply them in your daily life.

I want to thank you for trusting me enough to pick up this book. Now, I would like to encourage you to turn that page...because you are worthy, I see you, and I am here every step of the way.

In today's rush, we all think too much—seek too much—want too much—and forget about the joy of just being.

— ECKHART TOLLE

CHAPTER 1

Week One — Strengthening DBT with Present Moment Awareness

Welcome to the initial week of our DBT expedition. Did you know that research has demonstrated the remarkable effectiveness of DBT in enhancing emotional regulation and interpersonal skills? But before we immerse ourselves in this transformative therapy, let me divulge a bit of my personal journey.

Growing up, my life was anything but ordinary. You see, when I was a young girl starting fifth grade, I began to notice even more things that set my mom apart from the other moms. What do I mean by that?

My friends would invite me over to their houses without a second thought. But for me, it was different. I always had that voice in my head asking, *"I wonder what version of my mom we'll be walking in to meet today."* Would she be mad, loving, angry, or paranoid? Would she yell at me about something for 20 minutes in front of my friends?

You see, up until I started noticing how other mothers treated their kids, I thought this was normal. My mom was amazing, loving, caring, and supportive...until she wasn't. That's where the issue was. I had no control over when that switch flipped.

As I grew into a teenager and young adult, I had to learn how to cope, and I didn't always make the best choices. My mom's impulsive decisions became more frequent. She'd rush out of our home and tell us she was 'never coming back' and not to follow her. Her risky behaviors escalated, like drinking excessively and then getting behind the wheel. She became fixated on prescription drugs, convinced she would find the magic cocktail to quiet the storm in her head. This led to more erratic behavior, like regularly keeping me awake on a school night to 'help with my homework' until 3am, or to tell my brother to please take care of me because she would die soon.

I grew up in a home that never felt safe, even though it was theoretically full of love. My mom told my brother and I all the time how much she loved us but then would turn on us because we 'hurt her' and 'don't actually love her.' I also struggled as I grew older because my mom couldn't bear to be alone. I always felt guilty leaving her. I never had sleepovers or went to summer camp because 'we are a family. Why should you leave?' When I finally did leave and found my own place after college, I felt unable to navigate regular day-to-day life. Every small event made me believe that doom was lurking around the corner. I vaguely knew this was the result of growing up with a mom who was different but I didn't know what to do about it. My mom hadn't yet started using DBT and I didn't know about it either.

It was during this challenging period that I accidentally stumbled upon a powerful tool: mindfulness. It was life-saving for me. Mindfulness helped me interrupt those negative thought loops, bring myself back to the present moment, and acknowledge that the past was the past and that I had control over my future. Mindfulness is a huge part of DBT, but I wouldn't discover that until later.

When my mom's behavior reflected on me, I would take some time and space for myself. I'd find a quiet place and remind myself that her actions were not a reflection of who I was. I could empathize with her, but I no longer had to live through it myself.

What is Mindfulness?

You might have encountered the term 'mindfulness' tossed around, but what does it truly entail? We hear it all over social media, but trust me, it is not just another trendy catchphrase. Mindfulness revolves around being completely in the present moment. It's about observing your thoughts, emotions, sensations, and the surrounding world without passing judgment. What does this mean? It means digging in deep to your thoughts and emotions, even those tough ones, and practicing grace and kindness towards yourself. The goal is not to sit in your 'stuff' just to end up with that negative loop of thoughts judging every action you've ever taken in this lifetime. When we are mindful of ourselves, we often find the reasoning behind why we do what we do. That is the key to freedom. Our freedom. Our happiness. Our calm.

I want you to imagine yourself behind the wheel of your car and, suddenly, you realize you can't recall the past few miles of your journey. We've all done it! Were those lights green? Did I run a stop sign? You were on autopilot.

Now, ask yourself the last time you found yourself in a conversation, but your mind had wandered far away, only half-engaged. It could have been your boss giving further instruction, or your spouse telling you about their day. Regardless, this experience can leave us in a vulnerable position of lying when being asked, "Did you just hear what I said?" It can be embarrassing.

Being inattentive can lead to feelings of disorientation, anxiety, and frustration when reality doesn't align with our expectations. Fortunately, mindfulness can allow you to regain mastery over your thoughts and emotions.

WORKBOOK EXERCISE: A 'Mindless' Skill

Now, let's get hands-on. Mindfulness is a skill, akin to any other, that needs to be honed through practice. Many of us find ourselves frequently operating on autopilot, a state of *mindlessness*. Consider these commonplace scenarios and respond below them with a personal scenario of your own.

You find yourself driving or traveling (even just walking) and you don't recall the experience or the routes taken. In the space below, describe your most recent experience of this in detail. Where were you going? What time of day was it? Do you know what had you distracted? Were you alone on your travels?

_____
_____
_____
_____
_____

In the midst of a conversation, you suddenly realize you're clueless about the subject at hand. In the space below, describe the most recent, or the most embarrassing, time this happened. Who were you speaking with? Was the topic of conversation important? Did the person notice you were not engaged, and if so, how did you explain it?

_____
_____
_____
_____
_____

While reading, you abruptly discover that your thoughts have wandered, leaving you oblivious to the content you just read. In the space below, describe the most recent time this occurred. Was the content you were reading important? Was it for work or school? Does this happen often, leaving you frustrated?

_____
_____
_____
_____

The list goes on. These instances may appear benign, but for individuals grappling with overwhelming emotions, the inability to stay present can have profound repercussions on their lives.

The Power of Mindfulness: What Skills

Imagine yourself as the security guard at the entrance of a concert, carefully watching the crowd entering and leaving. Now, think of these people as your thoughts. You're not stopping each thought; you're simply observing as it enters. This is the essence of observing—sensing and experiencing without putting labels or descriptions on anything you witness.

In the beginning, it might feel a bit tricky. Our minds have a habit of talking non-stop, commenting on everything. But with practice, you can gradually quiet that mental chatter.

The real challenge of observing is to embrace the moment without passing judgment, without labeling your thoughts as good or bad, pleasant or unpleasant. It's like gazing at clouds drifting across the sky: You lie on the grass and peacefully watch them go by. No need to label them; just let them float along.

WORKBOOK EXERCISE: Let It Be

Find a quiet space, close your eyes, and observe your breath for a few minutes. Don't label it as good or bad, too fast, or too slow. Your job is to just relax and breathe. After a time that is comfortable for you, I would like you to reflect in the space below about how you felt in that moment. Be honest. Were you able to focus without distraction? Did your mind wander easily?

_____

_____

_____

_____

WORKBOOK EXERCISE: Observation of the Senses

I would like you to go wash some dishes. This is less about doing a chore and more about observing the act. Pay attention to the temperature of the water and silky suds as they flow over your hands. Focus on each dish as you hold it. The texture of a glass, a fork. In the space below, I want you to reflect on how this experience made you feel. Was it calming, relaxing, soothing?

_____

_____

_____

_____

_____

_____

Quieting our minds and practicing observation can be hard, especially when we're dealing with thoughts that make us uncomfortable. Our natural instinct is to react quickly and get rid of these thoughts as soon as possible. But here's the beauty of observing: it helps us understand that thoughts, feelings, and sensations are like passing clouds—they come and go, never staying for too long. This practice can actually dial down the intensity of our emotions.

DBT has a term for this: having a "Teflon Mind." It's like experiences, feelings, and thoughts enter your mind and gently slip away, just like a fried egg sliding off a non-stick frying pan.

Now, sometimes when we observe, it might stir up painful emotions. That's entirely normal. Think of it as a form of exposure therapy for your mind. Gradually, as you keep observing these thoughts and emotions coming and going, you'll find yourself less entangled in their grip. It's a journey toward emotional freedom.

Describing

The next skill in mindfulness is describing. It's about putting words to what you observe, without judgment. Imagine you're washing dishes, and you say to yourself, "*The water is murky. The soap feels slimy in my hands. The dish is heavy.*" You're simply labeling the experience without prejudice.

WORKBOOK EXERCISE: Daily Journal

I want to encourage you to keep a journal for three days, noting what you do and feel without judgment. For example, you go for a walk and notice the fluffy clouds, a child riding a bike, the sound of birds, and so forth.

DAY 1

_____
_____
_____
_____

DAY 2

_____
_____
_____
_____

DAY 3

_____
_____
_____
_____

Participate

Participating is diving wholeheartedly into an activity and being fully present. It's like dancing skillfully, one with the music and with your partner. This skill helps you step back from your thoughts and realize you're okay in this moment.

> **WORKBOOK EXERCISE:** Mindfully Participating

Start by choosing something you do often, like folding the laundry or walking your dog. This time, I want you to try and pay full attention while doing this task. Below, I want you to comment on how it felt different this time. Did you notice anything new?

_____
_____
_____
_____
_____
_____
_____
_____
_____
_____
_____
_____
_____

Practical Exercises

EXERCISE 1: Without Judgement

Take a moment to contemplate a recent situation where you passed judgment on yourself or others. It could be an event, a person's actions, or even a personal decision. Take a moment to reflect on this situation and record your judgments in the space provided below.

_____

_____

_____

_____

_____

Now, let's shift our perspective. Take the situation you wrote down above and try to look at it without any judgment at all. Imagine viewing it from a neutral and objective standpoint, like an observer rather than a judge.

In this section, try to describe the situation in a way that focuses on facts, actions, and observable details without incorporating any personal opinions or criticisms.

_____

_____

_____

_____

_____

EXERCISE 2: One-Mindfully

Select a straightforward task, such as washing dishes.

Rather than juggling multiple tasks or allowing your mind to wander, devote your complete focus to the task at hand. Feel the water's temperature, the texture of the dishes. Feel the bubbles and the rhythm of your movements. In the space below, I would like you to write about how this task felt different this time in comparison to previous times.

_____
_____
_____
_____
_____

EXERCISE 3: Effectively

In the space below, reflect on a situation where you reacted impulsively or ineffectively due to overwhelming emotions. For example, maybe you had a fight with your spouse the night before, yet you blew up at a coworker because those emotions boiled over.

_____
_____
_____
_____
_____
_____

Think about how the application of mindfulness could have empowered you to respond more effectively in that circumstance. Below, I want you to write how you would have handled that exact situation if you would have taken a moment to pause, and then been mindful.

_____

_____

_____

Remember, mindfulness is a skill that flourishes with practice. Commence with small steps, and, over time, you'll perceive its positive influence on your emotional well-being.

The Power of Mindfulness: The 'How' Skills

Let's explore the concept of 'one-mindfully' which is all about doing one thing at a time. It might sound simple, but in our modern, multitasking world, it's a skill worth mastering.

Imagine this: you're about to read a book. Instead of multitasking by scrolling your phone or watching TV simultaneously, you dive into that book wholeheartedly. Or when you're at work, you give it your all, without getting lost in making to-do lists or worrying about that upcoming dentist appointment. And when you're having a chat with a friend, you're fully present, not distracted by writing an email or preparing dinner.

I'll confess, I've been guilty of being 'that' friend, the one who's always distracted by scrolling on my phone while on a call. But let's talk about why it's essential to try and be focused on one thing at a time. We owe it to ourselves to give our full attention to what we're doing. We need to feel whole and undivided when we engage in these activities.

Mindfulness is all about the quality of awareness we bring to our actions and experiences, about being fully here and now. It's the practice of focusing on the present, on the task at hand, without being pulled in different directions by past memories, future worries, negative emotions, or anxieties. Let's not be too hard on ourselves; this skill can be tough to learn. It takes practice, patience, and a willingness to embrace it.

If you're struggling to concentrate on a single task, try letting go of distractions as they come. And if they persist, let them go again. Rinse and repeat! Concentrate your mind on the task in front of you. If you catch yourself doing multiple things at once, pause and choose only one to focus on. With time, this will become a habit.

For example, when I notice myself mindlessly scrolling while talking to a friend on the phone, I place my phone down. It's my small step towards improving, and yes, I admit, I still catch myself scrolling 50% of the time. But remember, we're all works in progress, and that's perfectly okay.

WORKBOOK EXERCISE: Train Your Mind to Be Present

Take a moment to reflect on your daily routines. Jot down instances when you notice yourself multitasking. Do you find yourself scrolling through your phone while having conversations with others? Perhaps you catch yourself eating while drafting work emails?

_____

_____

_____

_____

_____

If you ever find yourself multitasking, remember what we discussed earlier about letting go of distractions and giving your full attention to what you're doing. Here's a space below for you to jot down what distracted you and how you tried to stay focused. It can be enlightening to become more aware of these moments and to figure out what strategies are working best for you.

_____

_____

_____

_____

_____

Non-Judgmentally: Free Yourself from Criticism

Let's talk about judgments, something we're all familiar with. We tend to judge, whether it's others or ourselves, almost constantly. But here's the thing: judgment can create a hostile and negative environment, leading to emotions like shame, sadness, and guilt. So, what's the alternative? It's about taking a nonjudgmental stance, a way to explore those same old thoughts in your mind or observations in your environment, but from a different perspective.

Here's an example of what a nonjudgmental stance looks like: Sadness is like any other emotion, it isn't good or bad. Just because I'm experiencing the symptoms of sadness doesn't make me a bad person. Experiencing this emotion isn't a matter of being good or bad; it just is. It is normal and expected to feel sad.

WORKBOOK EXERCISE: Embrace Non-Judgmental Thinking

Let's try something the next time you're doing a regular chore, like folding laundry. While folding those clothes, practice observing and describing, in detail, what you're doing.

Here's what I'd like you to do: when you catch your mind starting to make a judgment, jot it down in the space below. Don't get tangled up in the judgment itself or worry that you've made one. Just recognize that your mind is passing judgment and then gently let it go. It can be as simple as, "Laundry is boring."

_____
_____
_____
_____
_____
_____
_____
_____
_____

Let's explore practicing mindfulness in situations that stir up strong emotions. It could be dealing with a difficult family member, a challenging coworker, or even a stranger at the grocery store.

Here's what I suggest: Pay close attention to your judgments, but don't let them overwhelm you. Treat your judgments like the tone of someone's voice—simply notice them without getting caught up in them. See if this approach helps you avoid impulsive reactions and stay calm.

In the space below, jot down the situation you faced, how mindfulness helped you in that moment, and how you might have reacted differently in the past.

_____
_____
_____
_____
_____
_____
_____

Key Takeaways for Week 1

- Mindfulness entails immersing oneself fully in the present moment without judgment.
- Inattentiveness can lead to anxiety and frustration.
- The 'how' and 'what' skills of mindfulness.
- The practice of mindfulness can enhance emotional regulation, distinguish judgmental thoughts, and facilitate wiser decision-making.
- Embark on the exercises provided to initiate the development of your mindfulness skills.

Feelings come and go like clouds in a windy sky. Conscious breathing is my anchor.

— THICH NHAT HANH

CHAPTER 2

Week Two — Finding Balance and Mindfulness

In this chapter, we're going to explore the three states of mind. I would like to really focus on the "wise mind," a state of being that can be incredibly helpful when dealing with difficult emotions and challenging situations. But before we get into all that, let me give you a quick overview of all we'll be covering in this chapter:

- We'll explore the concept of the wise mind and its three states: emotion mind, reasonable mind, and wise mind.
- I'll share a bit more about my own experiences growing up with my mom and her BPD traits and how mindfulness helped me cope then and now.
- We'll dive into various wise mind exercises, from concentrative mindfulness to generative mindfulness, and everything in between.

Let's get started!

Three States of Mind

Join me in the world of mindfulness and the intriguing concept of the three states of mind. As someone who can relate to the challenges you might be facing, I'm genuinely excited to share what I've learned with you.

Emotion Mind

Think of this as the time when your feelings are in the driver's seat. We've all been there, right? Those moments when you're super angry, frustrated, or profoundly sad. In emotion mind, emotions are in charge, and logical thinking kind of takes a break. We'll talk more about what's good and not-so-good about this state in a bit.

Reasonable Mind

This is when your brain goes all logical and factual. You might know folks who are super into data and facts; they're hanging out in reasonable mind. Guess what? We all have this state too. It's like having Google in your noggin, and you can switch between emotion mind and reasonable mind.

Now, here's the cool part. DBT has its eyes on something called wise mind. It's like finding that perfect balance, the best of both worlds. It's like mixing emotion mind and reasonable mind, with a sprinkle of intuition. DBT really likes intuition—it's like your gut feeling or just knowing something without needing loads of proof.

But let's dig deeper into these states:

- **Emotion Mind:** When emotions are in control, it's like a rollercoaster. We've all had our ups and downs with this. You may react quickly in situations where you feel fear or anger. It is possible you may want to lash out or hurt who hurt you. You could find yourself acting impulsively or on urges.
- **Reasonable Mind:** This is the logical, data-driven side. Some people live here most of the time, and it can be good and bad. You can feel cut off from your emotions in this space, often feeling numb. If you act out, you will often give excuses for this

behavior. In those difficult situations, you will shut off that emotional part of your brain that wants to acknowledge what is happening and end up in denial. If your emotions try to well up, you will try to minimize them.

- **Wise Mind:** This is the fantastic mix. It's having this deep sense of knowing. Ever look back and think, "When did I make a decision that just felt right?" That's wise mind at work. It's like having your very own unique compass. You will have that keen ability to think both logically and emotionally at the same time. The other great thing is the ability to see things from not only your own perspective. You will see situations from all points of view.

Remember, wise mind is personal. Nobody else can peek into your wise mind, and it's not something you can always explain with loads of facts and numbers. It's about trusting that deep sense of knowing inside you.

Key points to keep in mind:

- We've got three states of mind: wise mind, emotion mind, and reasonable mind.
- Wise mind is the goal in DBT, and it's all about following your intuition.
- Your wise mind is like your secret superpower; it belongs to you.

My Mom and Mindfulness

Growing up, I always knew my mom loved me. But she was on her own emotional rollercoaster, and I was often riding it with her. She could go from showering me with love and affection to seeing me as the most selfish person on Earth in a matter of minutes. Her outbursts of anger were frequent, and she often talked about feeling empty and even threatened suicide quite a few times. She had this constant fear that I didn't love her enough. She had this constant fear that nobody loved her at all.

One mindfulness technique I unintentionally adapted was what I called "Mom Pause." Whenever things got intense, I would sometimes take a deep breath, close my eyes for a moment, and then start again, more calmly. It was as if I was briefly tapping into my wise mind without even realizing it. This pause allowed me to step back from my overwhelming emotions—most that I couldn't name at that age—and think more rationally, at least for a moment. It was my way of coping with the turmoil inside my mom.

I learned that even in the toughest situations, finding moments of mindfulness can make a significant difference in your emotional well-being.

Wise Mind Exercises

Now, let's explore some practical wise mind exercises that can help you find that inner balance.

The Stone and The Blue Lake

Close your eyes and picture yourself beside a crystal-clear, serene lake on a beautiful, sunlit day. The air is fresh, carrying a gentle breeze that softly caresses your cheek. Now, imagine transforming into a tiny, feather-light flake of stone. You're as flat as a pancake and weightless. Someone has tossed you onto the lake's surface, and you begin a slow, tranquil drift through the calm, azure waters until you gracefully settle on the soft, sandy lakebed. Pay careful attention to your senses. What sights greet you as you descend? What sensations do you experience? Are you spiraling gently as you descend? As you nestle into the comforting sand below, take a moment to savor that sensation. Feel the lake's tranquility wash over you, and embrace the inner calm and quiet. Now, take a deep breath, visualizing your ascent towards the surface, drawing closer and closer to the warming sun, feeling yourself grow lighter and lighter. What emotions or sensations emerge within you during this journey? Use the space below to jot down your responses. Engaging mindfully with your surroundings can be a grounding and centering experience.

_____

_____

_____

_____

_____

_____

_____

Box Breathing

1. **Find a comfortable position.** Sit or lie down in a comfortable position. You can close your eyes if it helps you concentrate.
2. **Inhale (count of four).** Begin by taking a slow, deep breath in through your nose, counting to four as you inhale. Imagine filling your lungs from the bottom to the top, allowing your abdomen to rise.
3. **Hold (count of four).** Once you've inhaled fully, hold your breath for a count of four. During this pause, focus on the stillness and the sensation of holding your breath.
4. **Exhale (count of four).** Slowly release your breath through your mouth, counting to four as you exhale. Empty your lungs completely, feeling the tension leave your body.

5. **Pause (count of four).** After exhaling, maintain a count of four before taking your next breath. This moment of stillness allows you to prepare for the next cycle.
6. **Repeat.** Continue this rhythmic cycle of inhaling for four counts, holding for four counts, exhaling for four counts, and pausing for four counts. Repeat for several cycles, or as long as you like.

Make sure your breaths are slow and controlled. The goal is to calm your nervous system, so avoid rushed or shallow breathing.

Box breathing can be done virtually anywhere and is particularly useful in moments of stress, anxiety, or when you need to regain focus and composure. Like any relaxation technique, box breathing becomes more effective with practice. Consider incorporating it into your daily routine or during stressful situations.

Pay close attention to your breath throughout the process. Use the space below to write down what you notice about the sensation of air entering and leaving your body. Maintain an equal count for each phase of the breath (four counts for inhale, hold, exhale, and pause). This balance is a key aspect of box breathing.

_____
_____
_____
_____
_____
_____
_____

5-7-8 Breathing

1. Sit or lie down in a comfortable position. You can close your eyes if you prefer, but it's not necessary.
2. Take a deep breath in through your nose, allowing your abdomen to expand as you fill your lungs. Exhale slowly and completely through your mouth, letting go of any tension or stress with each breath. This is a preparatory breath.
3. Close your mouth and inhale quietly through your nose to the count of five. Imagine drawing in calm, positive energy as you breathe in. Focus on the sensation of the air entering your nostrils and filling your lungs.
4. After your inhalation, hold your breath for a count of seven. During this pause, try to remain still and relaxed. This holding phase allows your body to absorb the oxygen.
5. Slowly exhale through your mouth, counting to eight as you release the breath. Imagine expelling any tension, stress, or negativity from your body with each breath out. Focus on the sensation of your breath leaving your body.
6. This completes one cycle of 5-7-8 breathing. Begin again by inhaling through your nose to the count of five, holding for seven counts, and exhaling through your mouth for eight counts. Continue this cycle for four full breaths.
7. To experience the full benefits of 5-7-8 breathing, practice it for several cycles (four breaths in each cycle) or as long as you like. You can gradually increase the number of cycles as you become more comfortable with the technique.

Keep your body relaxed throughout the exercise, especially your shoulders and neck. Be sure to pay close attention to your breath and the counting. Let go of distracting thoughts.

The 5-7-8 breathing exercise is a valuable tool for promoting relaxation and reducing anxiety. By controlling your breath and engaging in this practice, you can create a sense of calm and balance in your life. Jot down how you felt before beginning this exercise and how you felt after. Did you notice tension decreasing? Do you feel more relaxed?

_____
_____
_____
_____
_____
_____

Asking Wise Mind a Question

When you encounter a situation where you're feeling stuck or uncertain, seek out a peaceful and quiet space. Take a deep breath in and within your mind, posing the question, "What would my wise mind do or say?" As you exhale, be attentive and receptive, listening for the answer. It's crucial to emphasize that this is a moment for active listening, not attempting to provide the answer yourself. Go through this process a few times. If you don't receive a clear response, don't worry; you can try again later.

Concentrative Mindfulness (Meditation)

Imagine it's a quiet evening, and you're sitting comfortably in your favorite spot at home. You decide to try concentrative mindfulness meditation. This technique involves directing your full attention to a single point of focus, like a flickering candle or a gentle stream. It's like zooming in on a single frame in the movie of your mind.

Here's how you can practice it (Compitus, 2020):

1. **Select your point of focus.** Begin by choosing your 'anchor'. It could be a flickering candle, a flowing stream, or anything that captures your interest and can hold your attention. Your anchor is your entry point into the present moment.
2. **Find a comfortable space.** Be sure to find a comfortable place to sit. You can use a cushion, chair, or simply sit on the floor. Ensure you're in a quiet place where you won't be easily distracted.
3. **Gently close your eyes (optional).** Closing your eyes can help reduce visual distractions, but it's not necessary. If you prefer to keep your eyes open, that's perfectly fine too.
4. **Begin observing.** Now, start observing your chosen focal point. If it's a candle, watch the flame dance and flicker. If it's a stream, observe the movement of the water, the ripples, and reflections. Let your attention rest there.
5. **Focus your thoughts.** You can expect your mind to wander, and that's okay; it's what minds tend to do. When you notice your thoughts drifting away, gently and without judgment, bring your attention back to your chosen point of focus. It's like guiding a wandering puppy back to its spot.
6. **Breathe naturally.** While you observe your focal point, let your breathing be natural. There's no need to control it. Your breath can serve as a gentle reminder of the present moment.
7. **Be patient and persistent.** Concentrative mindfulness takes practice. Your mind might resist staying focused at first, but that's normal. Be patient with yourself. Each time you bring your attention back, it's a small victory.
8. **Set a timer.** If you're new to meditation, you can start with just a few minutes and gradually increase the duration as you become more comfortable with the practice.

Generative Mindfulness (Loving Kindness)

I want you to picture yourself in your happy place. Maybe it is a sandy beach hearing the waves crash on the shore. Maybe it is in your pajamas nestled in your cozy bed. It's now time to go down a path of warmth and compassion. This is the essence of loving-kindness meditation, a practice that allows you to send out well-wishes and love to someone special in your life.

Here's how you can practice it (Compitus, 2020):

1. **Find a peaceful place.** Begin by finding a quiet and comfortable place to sit or lie down. Ensure you won't be disturbed during your meditation.
2. **Close your eyes (optional).** You can choose to close your eyes to minimize distractions, but it's perfectly fine to keep them open if you prefer.
3. **Take a few deep breaths.** Start with a few deep, calming breaths to center yourself. Feel the sensation of each breath as you inhale and exhale.
4. **Visualize someone you love.** Bring to mind someone you care deeply about. It could be a family member, friend, or even a beloved pet. Picture their face, imagine their presence in the room with you. This person could even be you!
5. **Offer loving-kindness.** As you focus on this person, silently repeat well-wishes for their well-being. You might say something like, "May they be safe, may they feel loved, may they be at peace." These phrases convey your genuine desires for their happiness and tranquility.
6. **Feel the emotions.** As you continue to send these wishes, try to genuinely connect with the feelings of love and care you have for this person. Let those emotions fill your heart.

7. **Extend the wishes.** After some time, you can expand your well-wishes. Start by including yourself: "May I be safe, may I feel loved, may I be at peace." Then, gradually extend these wishes to others, such as friends, acquaintances, and even those you may have conflicts with. The goal is to cultivate feelings of kindness and compassion for all beings.
8. **Breathe mindfully.** Throughout the meditation, maintain your focus on your breath. Let it flow naturally and use it as an anchor to the present moment.
9. **Set a timer.** You can choose to set a timer for your meditation session. Start with a manageable duration, such as 5 or 10 minutes, and gradually increase it as you become more comfortable with the practice.

Receptive Mindfulness

You're sitting comfortably in a serene park, and your eyes are gently open. In this practice, you're going to engage all your senses to truly experience the world as it unfolds around you.

Here's how you can practice it (Compitus, 2020):

1. **Choose your spot.** Find a quiet place to sit comfortably. It could be a chair, a cushion on the floor, or even a cozy spot in nature.
2. **Keep your eyes open.** Unlike many meditation practices, in receptive mindfulness, you keep your eyes open. This allows you to take in the world around you.
3. **Start with your breath.** Begin by taking a few slow, deep breaths. Let the rhythm of your breath settle you into the present moment.
4. **Use your senses.** Now, start to use your five senses:

- **Sight:** Look around you, paying attention to even the tiniest details. Notice the colors, shapes, and textures of objects. See the play of light and shadow.
- **Hearing:** Listen to the sounds around you, both near and far. Be aware of the subtle sounds you might not typically notice, like distant birdsong or the rustling of leaves.
- **Smell:** Take a few deep breaths and notice any scents in the air. It might be the earthy aroma of the ground or the subtle fragrance of flowers.
- **Taste:** If you have a drink or a small snack with you, take a moment to savor it mindfully. Pay attention to the taste and texture as you eat or drink slowly.
- **Touch:** Feel the sensation of your body in contact with the chair or the ground. Run your fingers over different textures nearby, like the fabric of your clothing or the bark of a tree if you're outside.

5. **Stay present.** As you engage your senses, stay present and avoid getting lost in thought. If your mind starts to wander, gently bring your attention back to what you're sensing in the moment.
6. **Take your time.** There's no rush in receptive mindfulness. Let each sense exploration be a slow, deliberate process. Savor each moment as it unfolds.
7. **Appreciate the experience.** As you immerse yourself in the world around you, take a moment to appreciate the beauty and wonder of the present moment.

In this chapter, we've taken a closer look at something pretty cool: finding balance through mindfulness. We talked about those three states of mind: emotion mind, reasonable mind, and that special wise mind.

You've figured out that balance isn't about picking one mind over the others; it's about blending them all together like a perfect recipe. It's about trusting your inner wisdom and that gut feeling you have.

In our next chapter, we're going to tackle something important—distress tolerance: what it is, how it focuses on acceptance, along with some actual, helpful tips and strategies for practicing it.

Remember, finding balance through mindfulness isn't just a goal; it's a way of living. And with each step we take, we're getting closer to being the best version of ourselves.

Stay kind to yourself, and let's keep moving forward together.

Key Takeaways for Week 2

- Wise mind is the balance between emotion mind and reasonable mind.
- Mindfulness can help you pause and find your wise mind, even in challenging situations.
- Wise mind exercises include breathing techniques, asking wise mind for guidance, and various forms of mindfulness meditation.

> *Out of suffering have emerged the strongest souls; the most massive characters are seared with scars.*
>
> — KHALIL GIBRAN

CHAPTER 3

Week Three — Distress Tolerance

In this chapter, we're diving deep into the world of Distress Tolerance. As someone who not only grew up with a mom who had a tough time managing her emotions, but who's struggled with anxiety and panic myself, I get it. Life can throw some seriously challenging situations our way, and sometimes, it feels like we're drowning in a sea of emotions. But don't worry; I'm here to guide you through it.

What is Distress Tolerance?

Growing up as the child of a mother with BPD, my childhood was a unique journey, to say the least. It was a rollercoaster of emotions and unpredictability. The one thing I never really learned to do was regulate my own emotions because most of my energy went into helping my mom deal with hers. It was an exhausting and often overwhelming experience.

Fast forward to when I was living on my own as an adult, and that's when the panic and anxiety reared its ugly head. All those years of focusing on my mom's emotions left me ill-equipped to manage mine. I found myself in a sea of emotions without a lifeboat. I had no coping skills, and I desperately needed to change that.

It was a pivotal moment when I realized that I needed help with coping. Accepting that fact was the first step on my journey toward healing.

This is actually when I found my mom's Marsha Linehan book of DBT exercises, the DBT Skills Training Handouts and Worksheets book. My mom hadn't filled out more than the first few pages, and wouldn't do so until later when she switched therapists. When I started reading through the dense book and I discovered distress tolerance skills, I can honestly say they changed my life. I saw a psychodynamic therapist for years after that, and talked about my past, which was helpful. Yet the DBT skills I learned have been even more helpful for me overall.

Now, let's dive into the concept of distress tolerance. Imagine it as that lifeboat you never knew you needed until you found yourself in the midst of a stormy sea of emotions. Distress tolerance is your ability to navigate and survive emotional distress without making things worse. It's your emotional survival toolkit, something I wish I had in my earlier years.

From a scientific standpoint, distress tolerance is closely linked to the limbic system, the part of your brain responsible for emotions. If you have low distress tolerance, you might easily become overwhelmed by stress and resort to unhealthy coping mechanisms (Compitus, 2020). Trust me, I've been there.

This is where DBT steps in to provide a lifeline. It helps us build healthier ways to cope with life's challenges. And guess what? It's working.

It's been working for my mom, who still has her rough days, but she's improved tremendously. Each day, I see her using her newfound DBT techniques to soothe her emotions. DBT has also worked for me – I have more confidence in my capacity to handle strong negative emotions and work through any kind of craziness that life throws my way. And that, my friend, is a monumental victory.

Distress Tolerance and Acceptance

Distress tolerance and acceptance go hand in hand, forming the foundation of emotional resilience and effective coping. These concepts are akin to the warm embrace of a friend when life feels overwhelming. So, let's look deeper into the power of acceptance and how it relates to distress tolerance.

Much like the practice of mindfulness, distress tolerance places a significant emphasis on embracing and acknowledging our current reality, warts and all. It serves as the initial stepping stone in our road to managing emotional distress effectively.

Picture this scenario: You're stuck in the middle of an endless traffic jam. Honking horns, frustration in the air, and there's not a thing you can do to change the situation. This is precisely where the magic of acceptance comes into play. Mindfulness and distress tolerance equip you with the strength to accept that traffic jam without letting frustration consume you.

Acceptance isn't about surrendering to life's difficulties; it's about acknowledging that some circumstances are beyond our control. It's the art of letting go of resistance and surrendering to what is. In essence, acceptance is the key that unlocks your ability to stay calm when life hurls unexpected curveballs your way.

Acceptance isn't a passive act; it's an active choice. It empowers you to face life's challenges head-on, armed with a sense of serenity. When you accept the reality of a situation, you free up mental and emotional space to respond thoughtfully rather than react impulsively.

In my own journey, acceptance was a hard-earned lesson. I spent much of my life trying to fix, control, or change my mother's emotions, only to realize that I couldn't. It was only when I accepted this reality that I could shift my focus to managing my own emotions and well-being.

Acceptance allows us to stop the futile battle against the inevitable and channel our energy toward what truly matters: our emotional well-being and growth. It's a cornerstone of distress tolerance, offering us the strength and resilience to weather life's storms while maintaining our inner peace.

So remember, acceptance isn't a defeat; it's a triumph of self-compassion. It's the path that leads you to a place of greater emotional strength and the ability to navigate life's challenges with grace and resilience.

TIPP Skills: Your Fast-Acting Rescue

Alright, let's get into those practical skills that can help you feel in control again! TIPP skills are your go-to tools when you need a quick emotional rescue. They work lightning fast, usually within seconds to minutes, to calm your emotional storm. You can do them anywhere—at work, school, in bed—without any side effects or cost. Let's break them down:

- **Temperature:** Ever tried splashing cold water on your face or holding ice cubes in your hands? Cold water gives your system a shock, instantly lowering emotional arousal. It's like hitting the emotional reset button. I always keep ice packs in my freezer for emergencies! If I feel I am having a rather difficult day I will grab an ice pack and occasionally put it on my face the back of my neck or hold it in my hands. This can literally remind me to cool down and can stop panic or anger in their tracks.

- **Intense Exercise:** When your heart rate goes up during intense exercise, adrenaline floods your system, giving you that euphoric feeling. It's hard to feel distressed when you're elated. I swear by this one; even doing jumping jacks in a bathroom stall can work wonders if you're not at home and are desperate to calm down. Try counting the jumping jacks—even in your head—to add that distraction component.
- **Paced Breathing:** Slow, controlled breathing through your nose (count to two; hold your breath; count to three; exhale through your mouth; count to five) can help you regain control. It's like taking charge of your body's panic button.
- **Paired Muscle Relaxation (PMR):** Tense and relax muscle pairs while breathing in and out. PMR teaches you to calm your body, to then calm your mind. It's an excellent practice for mindfulness and self-awareness.

Once you have completed the exercise, take some time to reflect on any thoughts, feelings, or emotions that may have come up during it. Did you find any of these were helpful? Will you keep some in your toolbox? If yes, why?

_____

_____

_____

_____

_____

_____

_____

_____

Five Senses Exercise

Use this exercise as a simple, versatile way to practice mindfulness throughout the day. Aim to be fully present in the moment, especially when formal mindfulness practices like meditation aren't feasible. This exercise helps you become attuned to your five senses.

- **Sight:** Without thinking much at all, what are the first five things you can see?
    - Look around and focus on five things you wouldn't typically pay attention to, such as a shadow or a small crack in the concrete.
- **Taste:** Focus on one thing you can taste right now.
    - It could be taking a sip of your coffee, savoring a piece of chocolate, or simply noticing the taste in your mouth.
- **Touch:** Bring your awareness to four things you can feel.
    - Pay attention to the texture of your clothing, the sensation of the breeze on your skin, or the smooth surface of a table under your hands.
- **Smell:** Tune your senses to two things you can smell.
    - Delve into scents you might usually overlook, whether they're pleasant or unpleasant. Maybe it's the scent of pine trees in the breeze or the aroma of a nearby cafe.
- **Hearing:** Tune in to three things you can hear.
    - Listen to the sounds of your surroundings. Whether it's a bird singing, the hum of a refrigerator, or faint traffic noises nearby, be present and take it all in.

This exercise is a quick and effective way to anchor yourself in the present moment and promote mindfulness, even during the busiest of days. Once you have had a chance to try this one out, reflect below how it worked for you. What about after practicing it a few times? Will you add this one to your toolbox?

_____
_____
_____
_____
_____
_____
_____
_____

STOP Method

The STOP method is a simple and effective technique that can be used to manage and navigate through intense emotional situations. It's designed to help you gain better control over your emotions and make more thoughtful and rational decisions. Let's break down each step of the STOP method:

1. **Stop:** The first step involves recognizing when you are experiencing strong emotions, such as anger, frustration, anxiety, or even excitement. Instead of immediately reacting to these emotions, you pause and intentionally stop whatever you are doing or about to do. This pause is crucial because it interrupts the automatic response that often accompanies strong emotions.
2. **Take a Step Back:** Once you've paused, the next step is to mentally and emotionally distance yourself from the situation. This can be done by taking a literal step back physically or by

creating mental space. By doing so, you give yourself a moment to detach from the immediate intensity of the emotions and gain a broader perspective.

3. **Observe:** With some emotional distance established, the next step is to observe your thoughts, feelings, and bodily sensations without judgment. This means being aware of what is happening within you without trying to change or suppress your emotions. It's about accepting that you have these feelings and acknowledging them without criticism.

4. **Proceed Mindfully:** After you've observed your emotions and gained a better understanding of them, you can proceed with a more mindful and intentional response. This step involves making a conscious choice about how you want to react to the situation based on your observations and your values. Instead of reacting impulsively, you respond with greater awareness and control.

Here are some key benefits of using the STOP method:

- **Emotional Regulation:** It helps you regulate your emotions by preventing impulsive reactions and giving you the space to decide how you want to respond.
- **Conflict Resolution:** It can be particularly useful in conflict situations, allowing you to approach conflicts with a calmer and more rational mindset.
- **Better Decision-making:** By taking a step back and observing your emotions, you're more likely to make decisions that align with your long-term goals and values rather than short-term emotional impulses.

- **Stress Reduction:** The method can reduce stress by preventing the buildup of negative emotions and helping you manage them more effectively.
- **Improved Communication:** It can enhance communication by allowing you to respond thoughtfully and empathetically in conversations, rather than reacting defensively or emotionally.

Cope Ahead Strategy

This strategy is used to help you prepare for and manage challenging situations effectively. It involves anticipating difficult situations, identifying potential emotional and behavioral reactions, and developing coping strategies in advance to reduce distress and improve problem-solving abilities. Here's a step-by-step guide and a workbook exercise to help you practice this strategy:

Step 1: Identify a challenging situation. Think of a specific situation or event that you anticipate will be challenging for you in the near future. It could be a social event, a work-related issue, or a personal situation. In the space below, write down a brief description of the situation, including when and where it will occur.

Example: Upcoming job interview next week.

_____
_____
_____
_____
_____
_____
_____

Step 2: List potential emotional reactions. Consider how you might feel in this challenging situation. List the emotions you anticipate experiencing. Be honest with yourself about your emotional responses.

Example: anxiety, nervousness, self-doubt

_____
_____
_____
_____
_____
_____
_____
_____

Step 3: Identify unhelpful behaviors. Think about how you tend to react when you experience these emotions. Are there any unhelpful behaviors or responses you usually engage in? Write them down.

Example: avoiding preparation, negative self-talk, procrastination

_____
_____
_____
_____
_____
_____
_____
_____

Step 4: Challenge negative thoughts. If you have identified any negative thoughts or beliefs related to the situation, challenge them with more rational and balanced thinking. Write down the negative thought and then counter it with a more realistic and positive perspective.

Example: Negative Thought: "I'm going to fail the interview." **Balanced Thought:** "I've prepared well, and I have the skills required for the job."

_____

_____

_____

_____

Step 5: Develop coping strategies. Now, brainstorm and write down specific coping strategies you can use to manage your emotions and behaviors in the challenging situation. Focus on strategies that will help you stay calm and effective. Give some of the ones offered here a try and see what sticks.

Example: Prepare thoroughly by researching the company and practicing interview questions. Practice deep breathing exercises to manage anxiety. Use positive affirmations to boost confidence.

_____

_____

_____

_____

_____

_____

Step 6: Rehearse coping strategies. Imagine yourself in the challenging situation. Mentally rehearse using the coping strategies you've identified. Visualize yourself handling the situation calmly and effectively. This mental rehearsal can help you build confidence in your ability to cope. Write down which tools you felt were most effective and why.

_____
_____
_____
_____
_____
_____
_____

Step 7: Create an action plan. Outline a step-by-step action plan for how you will implement your coping strategies when the challenging situation arises. Include specific details and timelines.

Example:

Two Days Prior to Interview	Night Before Interview	Morning of Interview
What did you find helpful in the research?	Practice deep breathing exercises.	Repeat positive affirmations.

Step 8: Monitor and evaluate. After the challenging situation has passed, take some time to reflect on how well your coping strategies worked. Write down what worked or if they helped you manage your emotions and behaviors effectively. If not, consider what adjustments you can make for future situations.

_____
_____
_____
_____
_____
_____
_____

Step 9: Practice and adapt. Continue practicing the cope ahead strategy with different challenging situations in your life. As you gain experience, you can adapt and refine your coping strategies to suit your needs better.

Remember that the cope ahead strategy takes practice, and it may not eliminate all distress in challenging situations, but it can significantly improve your ability to manage them. Over time, you'll become more skilled at anticipating and responding to difficult circumstances in a healthier and more constructive manner.

Crisis Survival Skills — ACCEPTS

ACCEPTS is another powerful tool in your distress tolerance toolbox. The skills help you manage distress by encouraging you to engage in healthy activities, seek support, reframe thoughts, and more. Let me walk you through how they work:

- **Activities:** Distract yourself with a walk or a hobby.
- **Contribute:** Talk to someone you trust about your feelings.
- **Comparisons***:* Remember past successes in managing anxiety.
- **Emotions:** Allow yourself to feel without judgment.
- **Pushing Away:** Shift your focus to a pleasant memory.
- **Thoughts:** Use positive self-talk to counter negative thoughts.
- **Sensations***:* Practice deep breathing to relax.

These skills can be a game-changer in managing distress, helping you avoid impulsive or harmful behaviors.

Surviving a Crisis with IMPROVE

Another valuable technique is IMPROVE, an acronym that represents a set of strategies to help individuals navigate through crises. IMPROVE stands for:

- **Imagery:** This strategy involves using your imagination to create calming mental images. When facing a crisis, you can close your eyes and visualize a peaceful place or scenario. This can help reduce anxiety and provide a temporary escape from the stress of the situation.
- **Meaning:** Finding meaning in a crisis can be a powerful coping mechanism. This involves trying to understand the significance of the crisis in your life and how it might contribute to personal growth or a deeper understanding of yourself. It can provide a sense of purpose and resilience during difficult times.
- **Prayer:** For individuals who are religious or spiritual, prayer can be a source of comfort and guidance during a crisis. Engaging in prayer can help you feel connected to something greater than yourself and provide emotional support.

- **Relaxation:** Relaxation techniques, such as deep breathing exercises, progressive muscle relaxation, or meditation, can help calm your body and mind during a crisis. These techniques can reduce stress and promote a sense of relaxation and well-being.
- **One Thing in the Moment:** Sometimes, focusing on just one thing in the present moment can be helpful. This strategy encourages you to concentrate your attention on a single task or activity, diverting your mind from the crisis and providing a brief respite from overwhelming emotions.
- **Vacation:** While it may not always be possible to take a physical vacation during a crisis, this strategy suggests mentally 'escaping' from the crisis by temporarily shifting your thoughts to a place or activity that brings you joy or relaxation. It's a way to provide yourself with a mental break.
- **Encouragement:** Self-encouragement is about being kind and supportive to yourself during difficult times. It involves using positive self-talk and self-compassion to boost your self-esteem and resilience. Remind yourself that you have the strength to get through the crisis.

These strategies collectively serve as a lifeline during times of crisis, enabling individuals to regain a sense of control and discover moments of tranquility amid the chaos.

By incorporating these elements into your coping toolkit, you can enhance your ability to cope with and ultimately overcome challenging situations. Each component of the IMPROVE technique provides a unique approach to managing distress, making it a versatile and adaptable resource for navigating life's crises.

Building a Distress Tolerance Kit

Building a distress tolerance kit is a valuable self-help strategy for managing emotional distress. Think of it as your personal emergency toolkit, filled with items that can provide comfort and help ground you when you're feeling overwhelmed. In the following steps, we'll provide a checklist and guidance to assist you in assembling your very own kit.

Understand the Purpose

Before you start gathering items for your kit, it's important to understand its purpose. This kit is meant to provide emotional support and help you cope in those really tough times. The items you choose should have a calming or soothing effect, and they can serve as reminders of self-care and resilience.

Create a Checklist

To help you get organized, make a checklist of items you can consider including in your kit. Keep in mind that your kit should be personalized to your preferences and needs, so feel free to add or modify items as you see fit.

Gather Your Items

Using the list as a guide, gather the items you've selected for your kit. These items can vary widely, depending on what brings you comfort and helps you manage distress. Examples might include:

- Stress-relief toys (e.g., stress balls, fidget spinners)
- Inspirational quotes or affirmations
- A comforting book or journal
- Photos of loved ones or happy memories
- A scented candle or essential oils

- A playlist of calming music or guided meditations
- Tea bags or your favorite snacks
- A soft blanket or plush toy
- Mindfulness exercises or prompts

Assemble Your Kit

Find a container or bag to store your distress tolerance items in. It can be a box, a pouch, a backpack, or anything that suits your preference and allows for easy access when needed. Organize the items neatly inside the container.

Personalize Your Kit

Add a personal touch to your kit by including a note or letter to yourself. Write encouraging words, self-compassionate reminders, or instructions on how to use the items effectively. This can serve as a source of motivation and comfort during tough times.

Keep It Accessible

Place your kit in a location where you can easily access it when you're feeling overwhelmed or distressed. Whether it's at home, in your car, or at your workplace, having it nearby is essential for its effectiveness.

Use It Mindfully

When you find yourself in a distressing situation, open your kit and use its contents mindfully. Engage with the items to help calm your emotions and regain your emotional balance. Remember that this kit is a tool for self-care and resilience.

Building a Distress Tolerance Kit is a proactive step toward managing emotional distress effectively. By assembling a kit tailored to your preferences, you can better equip yourself to navigate tough times and provide yourself with much-needed comfort and support.

That's a lot to take in, I know, but remember, this journey is about building skills that will empower you to manage life's challenges with grace and resilience. You're not alone on this path, my friend. Let's continue together.

Key Takeaways for Week 3

- Distress tolerance is your ability to manage and survive emotional distress.
- Acceptance is the first step in distress tolerance.
- TIPP Skills (Temperature, Intense Exercise, Paced Breathing, Paired Muscle Relaxation) provide fast-acting relief from distress.
- The STOP method and Cope Ahead strategy help you respond to distress effectively.
- ACCEPTS and IMPROVE techniques offer valuable distress tolerance tools.
- Build a Distress Tolerance Kit to support yourself during tough times.

We're making progress, and you're doing amazing. As we wrap up this chapter on distress tolerance, remember that life is not a smooth road and we should anticipate many "under construction" signs along our way. By cultivating the skills and strategies we've explored here, you are building a strong foundation for navigating the detours of life with resilience and grace. Now, as we venture into the next chapter on radical acceptance, you'll discover how letting go of resistance and embracing reality can be a powerful complement to your distress tolerance toolkit.

> *There is something wonderfully bold and liberating about saying 'yes' to our entire imperfect and messy life*

— ANONYMOUS

CHAPTER 4

Week 4— Radical Acceptance

I grew up with an emotionally unstable mother. My childhood lacked the normalcy and innocence most kids experience. While I knew she loved me, she relied on me to meet her emotional needs. I became her rock, her continual source of stability. Over time, her BPD diagnosis forced us into a challenging, codependent relationship, with deeply ingrained habits that took me years to break free from. I often felt like I was walking on eggshells, constantly navigating the unpredictable terrain of her emotions. She needed my constant validation to feel worthy because she grappled with chronic emptiness and a lack of trust in her own judgment.

DBT changed not only my mother for the better, but our relationship in the long-run. A huge part of that was exploring radical acceptance.

Understanding Radical Acceptance

Imagine a cozy scene where you're enveloped in the comforting embrace of a cherished grandmother. There's a feeling of warmth, security, and unconditional love. Radical acceptance is like that hug. It's a tender, nurturing embrace for your soul, a moment where you allow yourself to be cared for without judgment. It's a pivotal pillar of DBT, deeply rooted in the teachings of Buddhism.

The wisdom of Carl Rogers resonates here: He believed that acceptance is the first step toward change. Just as a seed must first be accepted into the soil before it can grow into a mighty tree, you too must accept your reality before you can nurture the growth and transformation that you seek (Main, 2022).

Radical acceptance isn't about putting on a façade, pretending that everything is fine, or forcing yourself to agree with the pain in your life. It's not about denying your feelings or bottling them up. They are your feelings, they are your emotions and you are entitled to them. They are a part of who you are. Instead, it's something much deeper and more profound.

Radical acceptance is the art of acknowledging the reality of your situation without allowing yourself to be engulfed by the dark storm cloud of suffering that often accompanies it. It's recognizing that storms happen, but you have the power to choose whether you stand drenched in the rain or seek shelter. It is asking yourself if you are worthy of that umbrella. Then, asking yourself if you are worthy of that rainbow.

Here's the crux of it: suffering doesn't always stem from the pain itself; it often arises from our attachment to that pain. Think about a situation where you're confronted with something beyond your control—perhaps the loss of a loved one or your job. In those moments, grief, sadness, and disappointment are natural and valid emotions. But clinging tightly to these emotions and resisting acceptance inadvertently prolongs our suffering. It's like standing under that metaphorical storm cloud for years, soaked to the skin without an umbrella.

Radical acceptance isn't about saying, "I'm okay with this pain." It's about freeing ourselves from the chains of suffering. It's the courageous choice to step out from under that storm cloud, even when you're knee-deep in rain. It's about understanding that you deserve sunshine, even when the sky seems perpetually gray.

In essence, Radical Acceptance is a profound act of self-compassion. It's choosing hope by accepting things as they are, even when they appear impossibly tough. It's not merely choosing an umbrella; it's about realizing that you are worthy of basking in the warmth of the sun. It's a radical shift from enduring suffering to embracing life with open arms, even in the face of adversity.

Recognizing the Signs of Non-Acceptance

Before we dive into practical exercises, let's become detectives of our own behavior and emotions. Here are some signs that you might be resisting acceptance:

Thought patterns:

- "I can't deal with this."
- "This is not fair."
- "Things shouldn't be like this."
- "Why is this is happening?"

Emotions and reactions:

- Blaming yourself for everything bad that happens.
- Feeling stuck and powerless.
- Wishing things were different but feeling helpless.
- Holding onto anger and resorting to unhealthy coping mechanisms.

Relationship patterns:

- Constantly nagging your loved ones, hoping they'll change.
- Frequent disappointment in others' choices.
- Holding onto grudges and harboring resentments.

Do any of these patterns sound familiar? It's okay if they do; we've all been there. Recognizing them is the first step towards embracing radical acceptance.

The Roots of Radical Acceptance: DBT

Enter Marsha Linehan, a brilliant psychologist who introduced DBT in 1993 (Cuncic, 2021). This therapy was initially designed to assist individuals with Borderline Personality Disorder, often characterized by intense emotions. DBT teaches us that while we can't alter the facts of a situation, we have the power to change how we perceive and respond to them.

We discussed earlier how DBT emphasizes a delicate balance between our emotional and logical minds, creating what Linehan refers to as the "wise mind," that place where we can make thoughtful decisions, removing the overwhelming emotions that often cloud our judgment. Acceptance, in this context, means taking reality as it is so we can move forward.

Now, you might be wondering why it's so challenging to accept things as they are. Well, rest assured, this is normal for many of us. We grapple with this, fearing that acceptance equals agreement or condoning the pain. Others dodge acceptance to avoid the inevitable discomfort it brings.

Remember, these feelings are entirely okay, but they're not insurmountable. Change is possible, but it requires practice and dedication. You need to want it.

The problem with resisting acceptance is that in our attempt to avoid pain, we inadvertently block out joy and happiness. Avoiding our emotions can lead to anxiety, depression, addiction, and a host of other mental health concerns. Instead, embracing calm acceptance allows us to process our emotions and take steps forward. Remember, you deserve the sunshine.

Practicing Radical Acceptance Exercise

Welcome to a hands-on exercise designed to help you enhance your ability to practice radical acceptance. Just like any skill, it becomes more refined with practice. Take a moment to reflect on each question or prompt and jot down your thoughts or feelings after considering them.

Identify Triggers: Pay close attention to situations or thoughts that trigger resistance within you. What tends to make it difficult for you to accept certain things in life? Write down your triggers.

_____

_____

_____

_____

_____

Embrace the Unchangeable: Remind yourself that in this very moment, the reality you're facing cannot be changed. Reflect on a specific situation in your life where this applies, and write it down.

_____

_____

_____

_____

_____

Recognize Lack of Control: Acknowledge that there are causes and circumstances contributing to your current reality that are entirely outside of your control. What are some factors in your life that you have no control over? Note them down.

_____
_____
_____
_____
_____

Actions of Acceptance: Envision what actions you would take if you had already accepted the situation. How would you behave differently? Write down these actions.

_____
_____
_____
_____
_____

Imagination Exercise: Close your eyes and imagine what life would be like if you fully accepted the situation you've been resisting. Describe this scenario in detail, noting how it feels.

_____
_____
_____
_____
_____

Emotional Exploration: Utilize relaxation strategies, mindfulness practices, or journaling to delve into your emotions regarding a challenging situation. What emotions arise when you think about it? Write them down.

_____

_____

_____

_____

_____

Physical Sensations: Pay attention to how your emotions manifest in your body. Is there any tightness, pain, or restriction? Describe any physical sensations you notice.

_____

_____

_____

_____

_____

Life's Worth: Consider that life can still hold value and meaning even when you're experiencing pain or difficulty. Write down ways in which your life remains meaningful despite challenges.

_____

_____

_____

_____

_____

Commitment to Acceptance: Make a firm commitment to yourself that you will practice acceptance when resistance arises in the future. What strategies will you employ to ensure you stay committed?

_____
_____
_____
_____
_____

By engaging with these steps, you'll gradually shift your focus away from dwelling on how things "could have been" and instead learn to embrace the present moment.

Empowering Statements for Radical Acceptance Exercise

Here are eleven empowering statements that can serve as your go-to tools when you find it challenging to accept certain situations and move forward. Keep these statements handy, so you can easily access them in the moments when you're feeling overwhelmed (Cuncic, 2021):

1. **Embracing Emotions:** "Resisting negative emotions only gives them more power. I choose to acknowledge and accept them."
2. **Past Acceptance:** "I recognize that I can't change the past. It's time to focus on the present and future."
3. **Accepting the Present:** "I have the capacity to accept the present moment exactly as it is, with all its imperfections."
4. **Strength through Difficulty:** "Even when facing difficult emotions, I have the resilience to endure. It may be tough, but I can handle it."

5. **Resilience:** "I will not only survive this, but I will also emerge stronger. The current pain is temporary, and it will fade."
6. **Managing Pain:** "Though this feeling is painful right now, I understand that I can endure it and come out the other side."
7. **Managing Anxiety:** "I can experience anxiety and still effectively manage the situation. My emotions don't define my abilities."
8. **Happiness despite Acceptance:** "I can accept what has happened and still find happiness in my life. The two are not mutually exclusive."
9. **Creating a New Path:** "Even in moments of discomfort, I have the power to choose a new path and make positive changes."
10. **Rational Decision-making:** "Staying rational enables me to make informed decisions and solve problems effectively."
11. **Action over Judgment:** "Taking the right actions is more productive than dwelling in judgment or blame. I choose to take constructive steps forward."

These empowering statements are your companions on your journey of radical acceptance. Keep them close, and remind yourself of their strength whenever you feel the need to embrace acceptance and move towards a more mindful and peaceful life.

Half Smiling Exercise

Half smiling is a powerful mindfulness technique rooted in DBT that can help you practice and strengthen your ability to engage in radical acceptance. It's a practical exercise that you can apply in various scenarios to develop greater emotional resilience and acceptance. Here's how to do it (Cuncic, 2021)

Half smiling involves literally forming a half-smile on your face, which can be a subtle and gentle upturning of the corners of your mouth. It may seem simple, but the act of half-smiling has profound effects on your emotional state and your ability to accept the present moment.

How to practice half smiling for radical acceptance:

- **Find a quiet space.** To start, choose a quiet and comfortable place where you won't be disturbed. Sit or lie down in a relaxed position.
- **Focus on your breath.** Close your eyes if it helps you concentrate better. Take a few slow, deep breaths to center yourself. Pay attention to the sensation of your breath entering and leaving your body.
- **Half smile.** Gently curve the corners of your lips into a half-smile. It's essential to keep this smile gentle and soft; you're not trying to force a big grin.
- **Observe your thoughts.** As you maintain the half-smile, turn your attention inward. Notice any thoughts or emotions that arise, especially those related to the situation you're struggling to accept.
- **Embrace your thoughts and emotions.** Instead of resisting or judging your thoughts and feelings, allow them to be present. This is a crucial step in practicing radical acceptance. Accept that these thoughts and emotions are part of your current reality.
- **Release tension.** Pay attention to any physical tension in your body, such as in your shoulders, neck, or jaw. As you half-smile, consciously release this tension, allowing your body to relax.
- **Stay present.** Continue to focus on your breath and the half-smile as you remain present with your thoughts and emotions.

Imagine that your half-smile is gently cradling these thoughts and feelings with kindness.
- **Breathe through it.** If you notice resistance or discomfort arising, take a deep breath and exhale slowly. This can help you stay centered and prevent you from getting caught up in emotional turmoil.

Scenarios for half smiling practice:

- **Dealing with past regrets.** When you find yourself ruminating about past mistakes or regrets, practice half smiling to accept that you can't change the past.
- **Facing uncertain futures.** If you're anxious about an uncertain future, use half smiling to embrace your anxiety and accept that some things are beyond your control.
- **Managing conflict.** In a conflict or disagreement with someone, half smile to accept the situation as it is and respond more calmly and rationally.
- **Coping with loss.** When you're grieving a loss, half smiling can help you accept the pain and sadness as part of the natural grieving process.
- **Dealing with chronic pain.** If you have chronic pain or illness, practice half smiling to acknowledge your pain while also finding ways to live a fulfilling life.

Remember, half smiling is a skill that improves with practice. The more you incorporate it into your daily life, the more effective it becomes in helping you achieve radical acceptance.

Willing Hands

Willing hands is a simple yet powerful technique that focuses on adjusting our body posture to enhance our ability to engage in radical acceptance. It communicates to our brain that we are in a safe and non-defensive space, encouraging a more open and accepting mindset. Here's how to practice willing hands:

Willing hands involves making deliberate changes to your body posture to signal to your brain that you are in a safe and receptive state. This physical adjustment can significantly impact your emotional state and aid in accepting the present moment. Try the following:

1. **Choose a comfortable position.** Find a quiet and comfortable space where you can sit, lie down, or stand, depending on your preference and the situation.
2. **Uncross your arms.** Start by uncrossing your arms if they are crossed. This simple act begins the process of opening up your body posture.
3. **Release tension.** Take a moment to release any tension in your body. Relax your shoulders, neck, and jaw. Breathe deeply and exhale slowly to further release physical tension.
4. **Open your palms.** Now, take it a step further by opening your palms. Here are some variations depending on your position:
    - If you are sitting, rest your hands on your legs or knees with your palms facing up.
    - If you are lying down, place your arms at your sides with your palms facing up, whether on the ground or a bed.
    - If you are standing, let your arms hang naturally at your sides with your palms facing front.

5. **Mindful Awareness:** As you adopt this open posture with willing hands, bring your attention to the sensations in your body and your emotional state. Notice any changes in how you feel and any increase in your sense of openness and acceptance.
6. **Stay present.** Whenever you encounter resistance, difficult emotions, or challenging situations, use Willing Hands to help you remain present and receptive. Allow this open posture to support your radical acceptance.

Incorporating this into your daily life can be a valuable tool for practicing radical acceptance. It's a tangible way to shift your mindset and encourage a more open and accepting approach to life's challenges. By unclasping your hands and opening your palms, you send a powerful message to yourself that you are willing to embrace the present moment with acceptance and grace.

Key Takeaways Week 4

- Radical acceptance is about acknowledging reality without judgment.
- Suffering often arises from our attachment to pain, not the pain itself.
- DBT teaches us to balance our emotional and logical minds for wise decision-making.
- Resistance to acceptance is normal, but it can be overcome with practice.
- Avoiding emotions can lead to mental health issues; acceptance allows us to process and heal.

If you have control over yourself, you have no desire to control others.

— MIYA YAMANOUCHI

CHAPTER 5

Week 5 — Emotional Regulation

My mom had her moments of love and affection, just like any parent would. But her struggles with emotion regulation meant that I often felt like I was walking on eggshells. She would tell me she loved me and I knew she truly did love me. However, her emotional instability led her to react unpredictably, in ways that didn't seem loving at all. This usually forced me to suppress my own emotional expression, thus inhibiting my natural growth and development.

I'm sure some of you can relate to this feeling, where you constantly find yourself trying to avoid any situation that might set off a storm of emotions in a loved one. You may have developed the skill of mind-reading, trying to preemptively understand their thoughts and emotions to prevent meltdowns. It's like living in a cage of control and engulfment, isn't it?

But the good news is that dealing with these emotions and these situations for a long time doesn't mean we're destined to a certain fate. We have the strength and the freedom to break free from those old patterns and rediscover our own emotional well-being. In this chapter, we'll explore what emotion regulation is all about, and how it can be a powerful tool for nurturing our mental health and happiness.

What is Emotion Regulation?

Emotion regulation is like the compass that guides us through the ever-changing landscape of our feelings. It's the ability to understand, accept, and manage our emotions effectively, without being overwhelmed or controlled by them. Just like a ship needs a steady hand on the helm during a storm, we need to learn how to navigate the turbulent waters of our emotions.

So, how can we achieve this? Well, that's what this workbook is all about. We'll explore practical exercises, backed by research and studies, that will help you become a master of your emotions. But first, let's take a moment to reflect on why this topic is so crucial.

Growing up, I often felt like I was living in two worlds. On one hand, there was my loving, caring mother who would hug me and tell me she loved me. On the other hand, there was the unpredictable side of her, the mother who would react explosively to the smallest things. These unpredictable emotions left me feeling confused, anxious, and, at times, helpless.

I know what it's like to be consciously or unconsciously 'trained' to tiptoe around, to anticipate someone else's moods, and to try not to provoke an emotional spiral. It's exhausting, isn't it? But as I learned about DBT and emotion regulation, I discovered that I didn't have to live this way forever.

The Three Thinking Styles

Understanding the three thinking styles is a fundamental part of DBT practice, particularly in helping you gain better self-awareness and the ability to manage your emotions effectively. Let's break down what they are exactly:

- **Reasoning Self:** Think of this as the part of your mind that acts like a wise and logical advisor. It's the voice that helps you look at situations calmly, gather facts, and make smart decisions. In DBT, you'll learn how to make this part of your mind even stronger, so it can help you when you're tempted to react impulsively or based on strong emotions.
- **Emotional Self:** This is the part of you that feels the really strong emotions. Sometimes these emotions can be overwhelming. In DBT, you'll learn how to handle these big feelings by acknowledging and accepting them, but without letting them take over and make you act in ways you might regret.
- **Wise Self:** Think of this as your inner wisdom. It's like having a wise and calm friend inside you. DBT shows you how to connect with your Wise Self by practicing mindfulness and emotion control techniques. This helps you make smart and kind choices, especially when things get tough.

Understanding the nature of emotions is vital in DBT, as it forms the basis for chain analysis. Here's how the three thinking styles connect:

- **Emotions are complex.** Emotions aren't simple reactions; they involve a series of interconnected events. DBT recognizes this complexity and helps us break down our emotional responses into manageable components.
- **Chain Analysis:** This is a structured process used in DBT to examine the chain of events leading to emotional reactions and problematic behaviors. It helps identify the various factors involved in an emotional response, enabling us to gain insight into our reactions.

Chain Analysis Factors

The main factors of Chain Analysis are the following:

- **Vulnerability Factors:** These are the predisposing factors that make a person more susceptible to emotional dysregulation. DBT teaches individuals to recognize and address vulnerability factors through self-care and skill-building.
- **Prompting Event:** This is the specific trigger or event that sets off the emotional response. Identifying the prompting event is essential in understanding why a particular emotion arises.
- **Interpretations:** Interpretations are the thoughts and beliefs that follow the prompting event. DBT encourages individuals to become aware of their interpretations and assess whether they are accurate or biased.
- **Emotion Name:** Naming your emotions accurately is a significant step in emotional regulation. DBT helps individuals develop a vocabulary for their emotions, which promotes better self-understanding and communication.
- **Biological Changes:** Emotions often come with physiological changes like increased heart rate or muscle tension. Recognizing these changes can signal the beginning of an emotional response.
- **Action Urges:** Emotions typically come with urges to take specific actions. DBT teaches individuals to pause and consider these urges before acting impulsively.
- **Behaviors:** These are the actions or reactions that follow the emotional response. DBT encourages individuals to evaluate whether these behaviors are effective or problematic.

○ **Aftereffects:** Aftereffects refer to the consequences of the emotional response and related behaviors. Understanding these helps individuals see the broader impact of their reactions.

Chain Analysis Exercises

Chain analysis exercises are practical applications of these concepts. They help us dissect and understand our emotional reactions by identifying each step in the chain of events leading to the emotion. By doing this exercise, we can gain valuable insights into our emotional patterns, develop healthier coping strategies, and work toward more adaptive responses.

By mastering these concepts and exercises, we can make significant strides in managing our emotions, improving our relationships, and leading a more fulfilling life. DBT provides a structured and compassionate framework for achieving these goals.

EXERCISE 1: Identifying Your Thinking Styles

Use the table below.

Reasoning Self	Emotional Self	Wise Self

Over the course of a few days, pay attention to your thoughts and reactions in different situations.

Write down the thoughts and emotions that come up in each column. Reflect on how each style influences your behavior and decisions.

EXERCISE 2: Exploring Chain Analysis

Chain analysis is a core DBT concept that helps us understand the sequence of events leading to emotional reactions and behaviors.

Use the chart below:

Fill in each step with examples from your own life, focusing on a specific emotional reaction.

Vulnerability Factors	Prompting Event	Interpretations	Emotion Name	Biological Changes	Action Urges	Aftereffects

Reflect on how each step in the chain contributed to your emotional response.

EXERCISE 3: Identifying and Challenging Interpretations

In the 'Interpretations' step of your chain analysis, identify any negative or irrational thoughts you had during the triggering event.

_____

_____

_____

_____

_____

_____

_____

Write down evidence that supports and contradicts these interpretations.

_____

_____

_____

_____

_____

_____

_____

Use the evidence to challenge and reframe your negative thoughts.

Notice how changing your interpretations can lead to different emotional responses.

Categorizing Your Emotions

Emotions can be complex but understanding them is crucial. Let's begin by categorizing emotions into ten key categories. These are the top ten emotions that are commonly addressed in DBT (*Do We Even Need Them? Your Guide to Understanding Emotions.*, 2017):

1. Fear

- **Definition**: Fear is that feeling of dread or unease that creeps in when you believe you're facing a threat or danger. It's your body's natural response to protect you.
- **Examples**: Fear might surge when you're walking alone in a dark alley, confronted by a growling dog, or anticipating a critical job interview.

2. Anger

- **Definition**: Anger is the fiery emotion that arises when you perceive injustice or frustration. It's like an emotional alarm bell, telling you that something isn't right.
- **Examples**: Anger can flare up when someone cuts in front of you in traffic, when you feel unfairly criticized, or when you witness an act of cruelty.

3. Sadness

- **Definition**: Sadness is the profound feeling of sorrow and grief when things don't go as planned. It's a natural response to loss or disappointment.
- **Examples**: Sadness might wash over you after a breakup, when you lose a loved one, or when you experience a setback in your personal or professional life.

4. Happiness

- **Definition**: Happiness is the joyful state when things are going your way. It's that warm, elated feeling of contentment and satisfaction.
- **Examples**: You may experience happiness when you achieve a personal goal, receive good news, or simply spend quality time with loved ones.

5. Love

- **Definition**: Love is the warm and affectionate emotion that connects us to others. It's a powerful force that fosters connections and bonds.
- **Examples**: Love is what you feel for your family, friends, partners, and even pets. It's that overwhelming sense of care and affection.

6. Guilt

- **Definition**: Guilt is the sense of responsibility and remorse when you believe you've done something wrong. It's your conscience telling you to make amends.
- **Examples**: Guilt can haunt you when you break a promise, lie to someone, or hurt someone's feelings unintentionally.

7. Shame

- **Definition**: Shame is a deep-seated feeling of inadequacy and self-disgust. It's an intensely negative emotion linked to self-worth.
- **Examples**: Shame may surface when you make a public mistake, reveal a personal secret, or feel like you don't meet societal standards.

8. Envy

- **Definition**: Envy is the feeling of wanting something someone else has. It often arises from a desire for what you perceive as missing in your life.
- **Examples**: Envy can manifest when a colleague gets a promotion you wanted, or when a friend shows off a new car you can't afford.

9. Jealousy

- **Definition**: Jealousy is the fear or apprehension of losing something or someone you cherish. It can be rooted in insecurity or possessiveness.
- **Examples**: Jealousy can strike in relationships when you suspect your partner's affections are drifting or when a best friend gets close to someone else.

10. Disgust

- **Definition**: Disgust is the strong revulsion or aversion towards something unpleasant. It's your body's way of signaling that something is unclean or harmful.
- **Examples**: Disgust may arise when you encounter spoiled food, witness an act of cruelty, or come across something physically repulsive.

Now that we've identified these emotions, let's explore primary and secondary emotions.

Primary vs. Secondary Emotions

Primary emotions are your immediate, instinctive reactions to a situation. Secondary emotions, on the other hand, are your emotional reactions to your primary emotions. They often arise from how you interpret or judge your primary emotions.

For example, imagine you made a mistake at work (primary emotion: guilt). Then, you start feeling shame (secondary emotion) because you believe you're a failure due to that mistake.

Exercise on Emotions

Think of a recent emotional situation. Write down the primary emotion you felt.

_____
_____
_____
_____
_____
_____

Now, reflect on the primary emotion. Did any secondary emotions arise from it? Write them down.

_____
_____
_____
_____
_____
_____

What triggered these emotions? Understanding the triggers can help you gain insight into your emotional responses.

_____
_____
_____
_____
_____
_____

On a scale of 1 to 10, rate how intense each emotion was during the situation. This will help you gauge the impact of your emotions.

_____
_____
_____
_____
_____
_____

EXERCISE 4: Create Your Emotions Dictionary

Creating your emotions dictionary can be a powerful tool in your journey to understanding and managing your emotions. Here's how you can do it:

Use the space below as a dedicated emotions workbook space. This will be your safe space to explore your feelings.

First, write down the ten DBT emotions: Fear, Anger, Sadness, Happiness, Love, Guilt, Shame, Envy, Jealousy, Disgust.

Next to each emotion, jot down your own definition or description. What does it mean to you?

- **Fear:**

- **Anger:**

- **Sadness:**

- **Happiness:**

- **Love:**

- **Guilt:**

- **Shame:**

- **Envy:**

- **Jealousy:**

- **Disgust:**

Write down personal examples for each emotion. Recall situations where you experienced these emotions and describe them in detail.

_____
_____
_____
_____
_____
_____
_____

Note what typically triggers these emotions for you. Is it a specific situation, thought, or person?

_____
_____
_____
_____
_____
_____
_____

By creating your emotions dictionary, you'll develop a clearer understanding of your emotional landscape, making it easier to manage and respond effectively.

In this chapter, we looked deep into the intricate world of emotions, exploring their many facets, from fear to happiness, and everything in between. You've learned that emotions are not just reactions; they are your inner compass, guiding you through the twists and turns of life.

Key Takeaways Week 5

- Emotions are natural. Emotions are a fundamental part of the human experience. There are no 'good' or 'bad' emotions; they all serve a purpose.
- Understanding is power. By categorizing your emotions and recognizing primary versus secondary emotions, you're gaining invaluable insight into yourself. This self-awareness is the first step toward emotional regulation.
- Embrace your emotional landscape. Emotions, even the challenging ones like shame and guilt, have something to teach us. Instead of avoiding or suppressing them, let's learn to embrace them as messengers.
- You're not alone. Remember, you're not alone on this journey. Many others are navigating their emotional seas as well. Your experiences are valid, and your emotions matter.

In the next chapter, we'll take these insights to the next level and translate them into even more practical tools.

Emotion-regulation leads to life-regulation.

— SAM OWEN

CHAPTER 6

Week 6 — Emotional Regulation Toolbox

We are about to begin another chapter on your path to mastering the art of emotional regulation using DBT skills. I know that the journey to emotional balance can be daunting, especially if you're carrying the weight of past experiences or dealing with overwhelming emotions. But know that I'm here to guide you, one step at a time.

In this chapter, we're going to explore the practical tools and strategies that DBT therapy has to offer that may be the best fit for you. Think of this as your emotional regulation toolbox: a place where you can find reliable methods to help you navigate the twists and turns of life's emotional rollercoaster. We'll sprinkle in some research-backed insights and relatable stories to keep things interesting, but our focus is on giving you actionable exercises and tips that you can implement right away.

I know that starting something new can be intimidating, especially when it involves emotions. If you're feeling hesitant or anxious about diving into this chapter, please know that it's entirely normal. I've been there too, and have dealt with multiple emotional challenges that wake me up in the night sweating with fear, so I understand the trepidation that can come with change.

Every step you take, no matter how small, brings you closer to a happier, healthier you. It's like building a sturdy bridge one brick at a time. And, today, we're going to lay the foundation for your emotional well-being.

So, what can you expect in this chapter? Well, I promise I won't bog you down with dry, theoretical stuff. Instead, I'll focus on practical exercises and real-world strategies that you can use in your daily life. Whether you're dealing with anger, sadness, anxiety, or just the ups and downs of everyday living, this toolbox you are building is designed to help you regain control and find that balance you've been seeking.

Using ABC PLEASE to Manage Your Emotions

I know dealing with overwhelming emotions is tough, especially if you've grown up in a challenging environment. I would like to offer you a powerful tool called ABC PLEASE. It's an approach that focuses on small goals (*Using ABC Please to Manage Overwhelming Emotions with DBT*, 2023). Let's break each component down further:

Accumulating Positive Emotions

Think of this as your happiness booster. When we're down in the dumps, we often forget what brings us joy, makes us smile, or makes us laugh. So, here's the deal: do things that make you happy. It can be as simple as chatting with a friend, listening to your favorite tunes, doing a craft you love, or even showing kindness to someone. These little doses of joy can help balance out those heavy emotions. Your mind and body collect these experiences, so don't feel guilty for experiencing them.

Building Mastery

Ever felt like life's spiraling out of control? Building mastery is like taking back the reins. Set some achievable goals. Maybe it's picking up a new hobby, tackling a chore you've been putting off, or daring yourself to step out of your comfort zone. Achieving these goals gives you a confidence boost and makes you feel more capable. The trick here is to make these goals achievable. Often, we convince ourselves that in order to snap out of a funk we need to climb a mountain, repaint the entire house, or declutter the garage. I suggest starting by making your bed. Yes, something that small. Each time you walk into your room, you will feel a sense of accomplishment. Next, try cleaning the kitchen or cleaning out that junk drawer.

Coping Ahead

Picture this as your emergency toolkit. Sometimes, you know situations that make you feel like a pressure cooker are coming. So, let's prepare! Practice some cool-down techniques like deep breathing, imagining a peaceful place, or telling yourself positive things. It's like having a shield to protect you from emotional tornadoes. For example, every time I have to deal with impending family holidays, I begin to stress weeks in advance. Not knowing how my mom is going to react to the way my kids behave or whether dinner is burnt sets my own emotions into turmoil. I lean into this coping mechanism now. I visualize the holiday going smoothly and I practice a few affirmations ahead of time. I also prepare some tactics in case the day takes a turn for the worst- if, in the midst of it all, I have to step out to practice my breathing, so be it. Protecting my emotional well-being is priority number one.

PLEASE for Your Well-being

Taking care of your body is so important. PLEASE is an acronym used to remind you to pay attention to your *physical* health. This acronym reminds us to: Treat **P**hysical i**L**lness, **E**at balanced meals, **A**void harmful substances, get enough **S**leep, and include some **E**xercise in our routines. When your body feels good, it's easier to manage emotions. This is a reminder that mental health involves treating the entire body.

Focusing on Small Goals

Okay, so the big picture can be daunting, right? That's where focusing on small goals comes in. Like we discussed in building mastery, break those huge tasks into tiny, manageable steps. Does your entire house need to be cleaned? Start with the smallest room. Allow yourself to feel that sense of accomplishment. Each small win boosts your motivation and helps you reach those big goals. It will make you want to continue on because, let's face it, tackling everything all at once usually ends in frustration and nothing getting done.

ABC PLEASE is like your trusty sidekick for managing emotions. It's about finding joy, setting and achieving goals, planning for tough times, taking care of your body, and tackling life's challenges one step at a time. Tuck this one into your toolbox and see how it fits into your life.

EXERCISE: Your ABC PLEASE Daily Plan

Think of this exercise as your personal roadmap to managing your emotions effectively. We'll create a daily plan that incorporates the ABC PLEASE skills.

Step 1: Accumulating Positive Emotions

Write down three activities or things that genuinely make you happy. They can be big or small, from enjoying a cup of tea in the morning to dancing to your favorite song.

_____

_____

_____

_____

Now, take a look at your daily schedule. Find pockets of time, even if they're brief, to engage in these activities. Make a commitment to yourself to do at least one of these things today.

Step 2: Building Mastery

Write down something you want to accomplish today. It could be as simple as making your bed or as challenging as starting a new hobby. Make sure it's something you can realistically achieve today.

_____

_____

_____

_____

Now, break that goal into smaller, manageable steps. If it's starting a new hobby, the first step might be researching what supplies you need or finding a beginner's tutorial online.

_____

_____

_____

_____

Find time in your day to work on this goal. Even if it's just 15 minutes, it's a step toward building mastery and regaining control. At the end of your day, reflect here about how you feel about your progress. Did this task make you smile? Did you feel relaxed or happy? What emotions surfaced?

_____

_____

_____

_____

Step 3: Coping Ahead

1. **Identify Potential Triggers:** Think about situations or events that usually trigger overwhelming emotions for you. It could be a stressful meeting, a family gathering, or a particular person.
2. **Develop Coping Strategies:** For each identified trigger, write down a coping strategy. For instance, if family gatherings trigger anxiety, your coping strategy might involve taking short breaks to breathe deeply or engage in grounding exercises.

Step 4: PLEASE

Assess how you're doing in the PLEASE department today. Are you feeling physically well? Are you maintaining a balanced diet? Have you been avoiding unhealthy substances? Are you getting enough sleep? Have you incorporated some form of exercise into your day? Make any necessary adjustments accordingly.

_____

_____

_____

_____

Step 5: Focusing on Small Goals

Create a short to-do list for today. Include small tasks that contribute to your larger goals or simply help you stay organized. Cross them off as you complete them.

_____

_____

_____

_____

By following your personalized ABC PLEASE Daily Plan, you'll be actively working toward managing your overwhelming emotions. Remember, it's okay to start small and gradually build up. Over time, these practices will become a natural part of your routine, and you'll find yourself better equipped to handle difficult emotions.

Feel free to come back to this exercise every day to adjust and refine your plan as needed. You can also start a separate journal with an ABC PLEASE plan that you can fill in every day. You've got this, and I'm here cheering you on every step of the way!

How to Use Opposite Actions

Imagine your emotions as a powerful force guiding your actions. Sometimes, these emotions can push us toward decisions we'd rather not make. In these moments, emotions tend to overpower our logical thinking. This is where opposite action, a valuable DBT skill, comes into play.

Let's break it down: When you're in the grip of a strong emotion, it often compels you to act in a specific way. However, instead of giving in to these emotions, opposite action encourages you to do the exact opposite.

Here's an example: Imagine you've just gone through a breakup, and you're overwhelmed with sadness. Your emotions might be urging you to stay home, away from all the reminders of your relationship. But with opposite action, you'd choose a different path. In this case, you might tell yourself to get out and do something positive, like going for a jog or seeing a movie with a friend.

Opposite action doesn't mean ignoring or suppressing your emotions; it's about recognizing and acknowledging your feelings. This emotional awareness is essential for implementing opposite action effectively. Instead of letting your emotions dictate your actions, you create a space between your emotions and your choices.

Can Emotions Control Your Actions?

Absolutely, emotions can influence your decisions. Opposite action helps you regain control. Often, people allow emotions like anger, sadness, or fear to hijack their logical thinking, leading to potentially life-altering choices. But here's the truth: You have the power to choose not to act solely based on your feelings. You can opt for a different course of action.

Like any skill, learning opposite action takes practice. Taking some time to review situations where opposite action worked or didn't is helpful. This reflection helps you understand what happened and refine your skills.

Remember, you're a human being with emotions, but that doesn't mean your emotions must always dictate your actions. By learning and practicing DBT skills like opposite action, you can make different choices and regain control over your life.

EXERCISE 1: Identifying and Labeling Your Emotions

Take a moment to sit quietly and focus on how you're feeling right now.

Write down the emotions you're experiencing. Be as specific as possible. Instead of just 'sad,' you might write "feeling overwhelmed and hopeless."

_____

_____

_____

_____

Now, let's rate the intensity of each emotion on a scale from 0 to 100, with 0 being no intensity and 100 being extremely intense.

_____

_____

_____

_____

Once you've identified your emotions, it's time to check if they fit the facts of the situation. Our emotions can sometimes be like unreliable weather forecasts, and DBT encourages us to fact-check them. Write down that same emotion and check if you feel the reaction fits.

_____

_____

_____

_____

EXERCISE 2: Fact-Checking Your Emotions

Pick one of the intense emotions you've identified. Write it below.

_____
_____
_____
_____

Now, ask yourself, "What is the evidence for this emotion? Does it fit the facts of the situation?"

Write down the evidence that supports this emotion and any evidence that contradicts it.

_____
_____
_____
_____

Now, let's talk about the magic of opposite action. Sometimes, our emotions don't fit the facts, or they might be ineffective in helping us achieve our goals. Opposite action is about consciously acting opposite to our urges when our emotions are pushing us in unhelpful directions. Write down what opposite action may help in this situation.

_____
_____
_____
_____

EXERCISE 3: Using Opposite Action

Write down an emotion you've identified that you'd like to change.

_____
_____
_____
_____

Think about an action that would be the opposite of what you feel like doing based on that emotion.

Write down the opposite action and make a commitment to take that action, even if it feels challenging.

_____
_____
_____
_____

Lastly, let's shift our focus to the positive side of life. It's easy to get caught up in negative emotions, but there are positive events happening around us too. Write down these moments to help counterbalance unwanted emotions.

_____
_____
_____
_____

EXERCISE 4: Focusing on Positive Events

Jot down at least three positive events or experiences from your day, no matter how small they may seem.

_____
_____
_____
_____

Write down how these positive events made you feel and the impact they had on your day.

_____
_____
_____
_____

Try doing this once a day for a week and over time, create a list of positive events that you can revisit during challenging times to help change your emotional state.

_____
_____
_____
_____

Remember, changing unwanted emotions takes practice and patience. Be gentle with yourself throughout this process. And if you ever feel overwhelmed, don't hesitate to reach out for support from those you trust.

Problem Solving

It's time to explore one of the most practical skills you'll learn in DBT: Problem Solving. It's one of the best tools you can have in your toolbox for dealing with life's challenges.

Life is always unpredictable and we find ourselves in situations we wish we could change. This is where problem-solving comes to the rescue. It's all about tackling problems head-on, making things better, and regaining control over our lives.

The Steps to Effective Problem Solving

#1: Recognize the Problem

The first step is realizing that you have a problem on your hands. Sometimes, we're so caught up in our daily hustle that we don't pause to identify issues. So, take a deep breath, pause, and recognize that something needs your attention. Write it below.

_____

_____

_____

#2: Define the Problem in Detail

Once you've spotted the problem, let's get specific: What's the situation? Who's involved? What's going wrong, or what's missing? Where and when did it happen? Think about how it affects you, what you do in response, and what you want to change. The more details, the better.

_____

_____

_____

#3: Connect It to Your Goals

If the problem doesn't mess with your goals, it might not be yours to solve. So, write down how this problem interferes with what you want to achieve. This step helps you clarify if it's worth your energy.

_____
_____
_____
_____
_____

#4: Explore Your Options

To avoid falling into the trap of black-and-white thinking, brainstorm at least three possible solutions. Get creative! More options mean a higher chance of success.

_____
_____
_____
_____
_____

#5: Consider the Consequences

Look at each option carefully. What could happen if you choose each one? Sometimes, it helps to gather more information to make informed decisions.

_____
_____
_____
_____
_____

#6: **Plan Your Steps**

Once you've picked an option, outline the steps needed to put your solution into action. Make a schedule for when and how you'll take these steps.

_____
_____
_____
_____
_____

#7: Evaluate the Results

You've taken action, and now it's time to see how the situation worked out. If you've successfully resolved the problem, pat yourself on the back! You've just shown off your problem-solving superpowers. But if problem solving didn't quite work, don't sweat it. Learn from the experience, go back to step 4, and keep refining your approach until you nail it. Write down three more possible solutions you could have used.

_____
_____
_____
_____
_____

Remember, problem-solving is a skill that gets better with practice. Be patient with yourself and stay motivated.

Five Options For Solving Any Problem

I would also like to review five options for solving any problem:

#1: Find a solution to the problem or make a change.

When we're faced with a problem, we need to do something about it. That means trying to figure out what's going wrong and taking action to fix it. So, we need to identify the problem. Once we've got a handle on what's going on, we need to ask ourselves a simple question: Can I do something to change or improve this situation? If the answer is yes, then it's a good idea to give it a shot. For example, let's say we're having issues with our partner. We might not be able to change them, but we can definitely change how we talk to them or interact with them. By improving how we communicate, we create an opportunity to work together and find solutions to our problems. It's all about taking practical steps to make things better.

#2: Change how you think or feel about the problem.

Sometimes when we're dealing with a problem, it's not just about fixing the situation itself; it's also about looking at how we think and feel about the problem. One way to do this is by using a few strategies. First, we can check the facts, like making sure we have the right information about what's going on. Then, we can try thinking dialectically, which means considering different viewpoints and finding some middle ground. And sometimes, we can act in ways that go against our usual reactions to see if it changes how we see things. Now, here's the interesting part. There are times when we can't change the situation to our liking, or maybe we're just not ready to take action. In those cases, we can choose to change our perspective instead. What does that mean? Well, it's about finding a way to go through a tough situation without making it worse and maybe even using it to become a stronger person on the inside. For example, let's say we're facing a challenge. Instead of trying to change the challenge itself, we focus on developing something inside us, like understanding, wisdom, or compassion. It's like using a tough situation as a kind of 'fertilizer' to help our personal or spiritual growth. So, it's not just about changing the world around us; it's also about changing how we see and grow from the challenges life throws our way.

#3: Accept the problem.

Alright, let's talk about how we can deal with a problem when it feels like there's no practical way to fix it, or maybe we're just not ready to make a change yet. One way to approach this is through something called "radical acceptance." Radical acceptance is like saying, "Okay, this is how things are right now, and I'm going to accept it without fighting it." It's the opposite of resisting or struggling against a tough situation.

Think of it like this: **Pain (how hard or painful the situation is) x Resistance (how much we fight against it) = Suffering (how much we end up hurting)**

When we practice radical acceptance, we're basically reducing the 'Resistance' part of the equation. By not constantly struggling against reality, we can actually lessen our suffering. For example, let's say your partner has a personality trait that drives you a bit crazy. Instead of hoping they'll change (which might not happen), you can accept that this is just part of who they are, and it's okay. So, radical acceptance is like letting go of the fight with reality and finding a way to make peace with it. It's a way to reduce unnecessary suffering when we can't change things immediately.

Stay Miserable

You can decide not to do anything to make your life or situation better. Instead, you might just stay stuck in feeling unhappy or uncomfortable.

Now, why would someone do this? Well, sometimes we're not ready to change things. We might not be prepared to see things differently, and we might not be able to accept the situation as it is. In those moments, it's okay to simply feel miserable. But here's the key: don't use it as a reason to be hard on yourself!

The important thing here is to stay aware. While you're feeling miserable, pay attention to *how* it feels. Does the situation stay the same, or does it maybe even get worse? How does it affect your thoughts and your actions?

Make Things Worse

There's one more choice we should talk about, even though it's not usually the best idea. Sometimes we all can do things that make the problem even worse or create even more, new problems.

Now, I have to be clear, this isn't a great option, but I mention it anyway so you're aware it exists. Most of the time, it's not what you want to do. Occasionally, you may choose this by accident, so I think it helps to be aware.

The most important thing is to pick the option that matches what you want to achieve and what you value. Think about the specific situation and what might happen if you choose each option. That way, you can make the best choice for you.

Perhaps the most profound scar left by my upbringing was the deep-seated belief that I was "too much" for others. The love from my mother had been inconsistent, a rollercoaster of affection followed by harsh criticism, rejection, or hostility whenever I sought her attention. I learned that expressing my emotional needs was dangerous and would only lead to despair and humiliation.

The ABC PLEASE skills I learned through DBT became my lifeline. These skills allowed me to regulate my emotions, establish boundaries, and assert myself without succumbing to guilt or fear, even when control and a real sense of self felt impossible.

Key Takeaways Week 6

- Focus on adding more positive experiences to your life for better emotional well-being. Use a short exercise to find and include positive activities in your daily routine.
- Improve your skills and confidence in different areas of life. Try a short exercise to identify where you can enhance your skills.
- Prepare for tough situations and emotions in advance. Learn cope ahead techniques through a short exercise to handle upcoming stressors effectively.
- Take care of your physical health because it affects your emotions. This means eating well, getting enough sleep, staying active, and avoiding substances that change your mood.
- Understand and change emotions that don't fit the situation, hinder your goals, or are too intense.
- Alter your emotions by doing the opposite of what your initial urges suggest. Practice this technique through exercises like identifying emotions, fact-checking them, and challenging your urges.
- Start problem-solving by clearly understanding the issue. Use an exercise to define and grasp the problem better.

- Explore five approaches to address problems: solving the problem, changing how you think/feel about it, accepting it, staying unhappy, or making things worse.
- Determine your desired outcomes; it's vital for effective problem-solving. An exercise can help you with this.
- Recognize the importance of brainstorming potential solutions and use an exercise to generate ideas for solving problems.

These concepts and exercises are valuable tools for improving emotion regulation, managing stress, and addressing life's challenges effectively. Practicing these skills can contribute to enhanced emotional well-being and overall resilience.

In this chapter, we've explored the powerful tools and techniques offered by DBT to construct your personal emotional regulation toolkit. We've delved into skills like Accumulating Positives, Building Mastery, Cope Ahead, and the importance of taking care of your physical well-being through the PLEASE acronym. You've learned to recognize and change unwanted emotions, using the transformative method of Opposite Action. Additionally, we've tackled the fundamentals of effective problem-solving, equipping you with the ability to define problems, set goals, brainstorm solutions, and choose the best course of action.

As we approach the final chapter of our journey through DBT, we'll explore the realm of interpersonal effectiveness. These skills will help you navigate and nurture your relationships, enhancing your ability to communicate, set boundaries, and maintain healthy connections with others. By combining the emotional regulation techniques you've acquired in this chapter with the interpersonal effectiveness skills in the next, you'll be better equipped to lead a more balanced, harmonious, and fulfilling life.

"

Communication is an art form that is crafted throughout our lives.

— ANONYMOUS

CHAPTER 7

Week 7 — Interpersonal Effectiveness

When it comes to improving our lives and finding that sweet spot of happiness and contentment, we're often bombarded with a sea of advice and self-help resources. It can feel overwhelming, like trying to choose the best ice cream flavor at an all-you-can-eat buffet. But if there's one skill set that stands out, it's our ability to communicate effectively and navigate the sometimes turbulent waters of human interaction.

Think about it: We encounter people from all walks of life, every single day. Some are family, some are friends, some are co-workers, and some are complete strangers. And while we don't need to become the life of the party or the world's greatest conversationalist for every encounter, we do need to find a way to connect, to communicate, and to get along reasonably well with others.

Now, here's where it gets even more interesting. For folks like us who may be grappling with mental health challenges like depression, anxiety, and/or BPD, the art of interpersonal effectiveness can feel like folding a fitted sheet. It's like trying to climb Mount Everest with a backpack full of rocks.

In this chapter, we're going to explore the fascinating world of interpersonal effectiveness. We'll dive headfirst into practical exercises and activities that you can implement right away.

So, get ready to boost your communication skills, strengthen your relationships, and enhance your overall quality of life. Whether you're a natural extrovert or an introverted soul, there's something here for everyone.

What Is Interpersonal Effectiveness?

Imagine a world where you can navigate your relationships with confidence, assertiveness, and empathy, all while respecting your own boundaries and values. That's exactly what Interpersonal Effectiveness is all about. It's the art of communicating and interacting with others in a way that's both respectful and assertive. This skill is like a magic key that can unlock better connections with friends, family, coworkers, and even strangers you meet on your journey.

Let's take a quick peek at some research and studies that back up the importance of interpersonal effectiveness in our lives.

Research published in the Journal of Positive Psychology found that individuals who practice effective interpersonal skills tend to have better relationships and, as a result, experience improved mental health (Ackerman, 2019). So, developing these skills can lead to a happier and more balanced life!

Another study from the Journal of Behavioral Medicine revealed that people who use interpersonal effectiveness techniques have lower levels of interpersonal conflict and stress (Wu et al., 2023). These findings highlight the real-world benefits of mastering this skill.

What Is Emotional Effectiveness?

So, what exactly is emotional effectiveness? Think of it as your secret weapon for navigating the often turbulent waters of your emotions and the emotions of those around you. It's like having a superpower that allows you to connect with people, solve problems, and achieve your goals, all while keeping your cool.

Let's dive into some practical tips and exercises to help you boost your emotional effectiveness:

Mindfulness of Current Emotion Exercise

Find a quiet, comfortable spot and take a few deep breaths.

Close your eyes and check in with yourself. Write down what emotions you are feeling right now. Be specific. Are you feeling angry, sad, happy, anxious? Rate the intensity of that emotion on a scale from 1 to 10.

_____

_____

_____

_____

Naming Emotions Exercise

Sometimes, just putting a name to your emotion can make it more manageable.

Here's a list of emotions. Try to identify the exact emotion you're experiencing:

- SAD, blue, depressed, down, unhappy
- ANXIOUS, worried, panicky, nervous, frightened

- GUILTY, remorseful, bad, ashamed
- INFERIOR, worthless, inadequate, defective, incompetent
- LONELY, unloved, unwanted, rejected, alone, abandoned
- EMBARRASSED, foolish, humiliated, self-conscious
- HOPELESS, discouraged, pessimistic, despairing
- FRUSTRATED, stuck, thwarted, defeated
- ANGRY, mad, resentful, annoyed, irritated, upset, furious

Write down three words or phrases that describe your emotion.

_____

_____

_____

Pros and Cons Exercise

Using the chart below, list the potential benefits and drawbacks of expressing your current emotion in the situation you're facing. This can help you make a more informed decision about how to respond.

Pros of Acting on Emotion	Cons of Acting on Emotion

Clarifying Your Priorities

In DBT therapy, we often talk about three essential priorities: objectives or goals, relationships, and self-respect. These priorities are like the pillars that hold up the structure of your life. Let's take a closer look at each one:

- **Objectives and Goals:** This pillar is all about setting and achieving your personal and professional objectives. It's about realizing your dreams, achieving your goals, and making your aspirations come true.
- **Relationship:** The relationship pillar emphasizes the importance of nurturing connections with others. It's about building and maintaining healthy, loving, and supportive relationships with friends, family, and partners.
- **Self-respect:** The self-respect pillar is all about valuing and caring for yourself. It's about setting boundaries, practicing self-compassion, and maintaining your dignity and self-worth.

Now, let's look at an exercise to help you clarify your priorities between these three pillars in different situations.

Prioritizing Your Three Pillars Exercise

Imagine you're faced with three different scenarios. For each scenario, jot down which pillar (objective/goal, relationship, or self-respect) you believe should take precedence. Don't overthink it; trust your initial instincts.

Scenario 1: You've been working long hours at your job, and your boss asks you to stay late to complete a critical project. You already promised your friend you'd attend their important event tonight.

Priority:

- ◯ Objective/Goal-
- ◯ Relationship-
- ◯ Self-Respect-

Scenario 2: Your partner is upset because you've been spending a lot of time on your personal project, neglecting quality time together. They want to have a heartfelt conversation about your relationship.

Priority:

- ◯ Objective/Goal-
- ◯ Relationship-
- ◯ Self-Respect-

Scenario 3: You've been feeling overwhelmed and exhausted, and a friend invites you to a social gathering that you're not particularly excited about attending.

Priority:

- ◯ Objective/Goal-
- ◯ Relationship-
- ◯ Self-Respect-

Remember, there are no right or wrong answers here. Your priorities may shift depending on the situation, and that's perfectly okay.

Take your time with this exercise and remember that your priorities can change over time. The important thing is to stay true to yourself and what feels right for you in each moment.

Levels of Intensity

Determining your intensity level is like having a volume knob for your emotions and interactions, and it is a vital skill to have. Growing up, and even into my late twenties, I'd often find myself unsure of how to respond to my mom's intense reactions and requests. I would swing from guilty and people-pleasing to angry and self-righteous. It became important to find DBT skills that could help.

The Emotion Thermometer Exercise

Imagine a thermometer with different levels of intensity, just like the one we use to measure temperature. On a piece of paper, create a similar scale from 1 to 10, with 1 being the coolest and 10 being the hottest. Now, let's practice:

- **Identify your emotion.** When you feel an emotion bubbling up, jot it down on the thermometer scale according to its intensity. For example, if you're mildly annoyed, mark it as a 3, but if you're furious, it might be a 9 or 10.
- **Rate your response:** Next, think about how you typically respond to this emotion. Do you scream when you're angry, or do you calmly express your feelings? Mark your typical response on the scale.
- **Assess effectiveness.** Reflect on whether your typical response matches the intensity of your emotion. Is it an overreaction, underreaction, or just right? This exercise helps you become more aware of your emotional responses.

The 10-Second Rule Exercise

Whenever you're about to respond to something or make a request, pause for a moment. Take a deep breath and count to 10 in your head. Use this time to assess the intensity of your emotions and whether they match the situation. After those 10 seconds, decide how to respond appropriately.

Studies have shown that individuals who practice emotional regulation techniques, such as determining their intensity level, experience improved interpersonal relationships and reduced emotional distress (Lavender et al. 2016). DBT, in particular, has been found effective in helping individuals with BPD manage their emotional intensity (Chapman, 2006).

So, learning to determine your intensity level is a skill that can save you from unnecessary stress and conflicts. Practice these exercises, and over time, you'll become a pro at managing your emotional thermostat. Remember, it's all about finding that sweet spot of just-right intensity.

DEAR MAN

One of the awesome tools we have yet to explore is DEAR MAN, and it's like your trusty sidekick when it comes to achieving your goals in conversations. Let's break it down:

- **Describe:** Start by telling the other person exactly what's happening. Stick to the facts and avoid adding judgments or emotions.
- **Express:** Let your feelings out in the open using 'I' statements. This is your chance to honestly share how you feel without blaming anyone.

- **Assert:** Get straight to the point and clearly state what you want or need. Be direct and specific so there's no room for confusion.
- **Reinforce:** Explain why your request is a good idea. How will it benefit both parties? And if there's a reward involved, make sure to follow through. It makes people more likely to say 'yes'.
- **Mindful:** Stay laser-focused on your goal. Don't let yourself get sidetracked or carried away by the conversation. If necessary, calmly repeat your point like a broken record.
- **Appear Confident:** Show confidence through your tone of voice and body language. Stand tall, maintain eye contact, and speak with certainty.
- **Negotiate:** Be flexible and open to finding middle ground. Sometimes, you might need to offer alternatives or scale back your request to reach a solution that works for everyone.

Now, when using DEAR MAN, you need to have a clear goal in mind. Think about what you really want or need, considering your priorities and time constraints. Don't hesitate to ask for help when necessary, even if you're feeling a bit overwhelmed. DEAR MAN can also be your go-to tool for seeking assistance.

Here are some common goals you might have when using DEAR MAN:

- Standing up for your rights so they're taken seriously.
- Requesting something from others effectively.
- Politely refusing unwanted or unreasonable requests and making your decision stick.
- Resolving conflicts with others.
- Ensuring your opinion or point of view is heard and valued.

It's important to note that even though these skills are incredibly helpful, there's no magic formula for always getting what you want from others. Some situations might not budge, no matter how skilled you are.

If the conversation turns toxic, you might even need to do a DEAR MAN within the original DEAR MAN to address the new situation. Describe the issue, express how it's making you feel, assert what you want to change, reinforce your point, and do it all confidently and mindfully.

DEAR MAN Exercise: Making a Plan

I know each and every time I had to confront my mother about anything, my anxiety grew. I found it helpful to make a plan ahead of time. Below, let's walk through a plan using the DEAR MAN method.

Write down your current situation. What do you want to tell the person? Remember to stick to the facts.

_____

_____

_____

_____

What feelings and opinions regarding the situation do you want to make sure they understand? We always want to believe they have no idea how hard it is for you to ask for what you want.

_____

_____

_____

_____

Write down exactly how you will assert yourself by asking for what you need or saying 'no' to a request clearly. What will you say?

_____
_____
_____
_____

Write down what the person will gain from this. What are the positive effects of getting what you want or need? How will *they* feel good for doing what you want?

_____
_____
_____
_____

Being prepared ahead of time can help you be focused on your objective. Remember to be confident, maintaining eye contact. Be willing to offer and ask for alternative solutions to the problem. Write down what you are willing to settle for or give up in order to gain what you want in the situation.

_____
_____
_____
_____

In this chapter, we learned that being awesome in relationships isn't just about being polite; it's about gracefully and assertively navigating the wild world of human connections. Plus, we unlocked the superpower of emotional effectiveness: how to handle our feelings like champs!

Remember, it's not about squishing your feelings into a tiny box. It's about letting them out in the right way, like confetti at a celebration.

We talked about the three amigos of every interpersonal showdown: your goal, your relationship, and your self-respect. Sometimes, these buddies don't play nice together, and that's when things get tricky.

We gave you an exercise to help you figure out your priority in different situations. Think of it as your emotional GPS, showing you the way when things get a bit wild.

In the heat of the moment, it's easy to go full-on fire-breathing dragon mode. We chatted about dialing up or down the intensity when you're dealing with stuff. Sometimes, you need a gentle breeze, and sometimes you need a hurricane.

We unveiled the DEAR MAN toolkit! This is your secret weapon for getting what you want while keeping your relationships sparkling. A quick recap:

- **D**: Describe the issues objectively.
- **E**: Express your feelings and opinions.
- **A**: Assert your needs clearly.
- **R**: Reinforce your point with benefits or consequences.

We gave you the homework to think of real-life examples for each one—soon you'll be doing them without even thinking!

And don't forget about **MAN**:

- **M**: Stay Mindful of your objectives and priorities.
- **A**: Appear confident (think superhero cape!) in your communication.
- **N**: Be ready to Negotiate like a pro when needed.

Key Takeaways Week 7

- Interpersonal Effectiveness is all about handling your relationships effectively while respecting both yourself and others.
- Emotional Effectiveness is understanding and managing *your* emotions in your interactions with others.
- Learn to gauge the appropriate level of intensity when responding to something or making a request.
- DEAR MAN is a powerful tool for getting what you want.
- Explore examples of each element:
  - Describe: Clearly state the facts.
  - Express: Share your feelings and opinions.
  - Assert: Make your needs known.
  - Reinforce: Offer incentives or reasons for the other person to comply.
- **MAN stands for:**
  - Mindful: Stay present and attentive during the interaction.
  - Appear Confident: Project confidence, even if you don't feel it.
  - Negotiate: Be open to finding solutions that work for both parties.
- Engage in short exercises to practice these elements and tie them all together for effective communication.

In the next chapter, we're diving into validation, gentle communication skills and some hands-on exercises. Your path to being a more confident social communicator is just beginning, so keep your motivation high, and let's jump into those exercises!

Empathy is a strange and powerful thing. There is no script. There is no right way or wrong way to do it. It's simply listening, holding space, withholding judgment, emotionally connecting, and communicating that incredibly healing message of "You're not alone."

-BRENÉ BROWN

CHAPTER 8

Understanding the Power of Validation

In this chapter, we're going to explore Marsha Linehan's six levels of validation and how they can transform your relationships, as well as the powerful GIVE and FAST skills that will help you navigate through life's challenges with self-respect and effectiveness.

The Six Levels of Validation

Marsha Linehan, the brilliant mind behind DBT, has emphasized the immense importance of validation. In fact, she believes it's impossible to overstate its significance. Whether you're trying to support someone you care about or learning to manage your own emotions, validation is your secret superpower.

Linehan suggests using the highest level of validation possible in any given situation. Let's break down the six levels of validation to help you understand how to harness this incredible skill (*Understanding the Levels of Validation*, 2012).

Level One: Being Present

Being present is about giving your full, undivided attention to someone. It's holding a friend's hand during a painful medical treatment, listening intently to a child's description of their day, or being there for someone when they're in need. When you're present, you're truly engaged, both with others and with yourself. It means acknowledging your internal experience without trying to escape or avoid it, even if it's uncomfortable. Remember, sitting with intense emotions is a brave act.

Workbook Exercise

Practice being present with someone you care about. Listen without judgment and notice how it makes them feel. Also, try being present for yourself. Sit quietly, acknowledge your emotions, and see how they affect your own mental state. Feel free to jot down any emotions that come through.

_____
_____
_____
_____
_____

Level Two: Accurate Reflection

Accurate reflection is like holding up a mirror to someone's feelings. It involves summarizing what you've heard from them or even summarizing your own emotions. But remember, it's not about being artificial or critical; it's about genuinely understanding and not judging. Accurate reflection can help emotionally sensitive individuals untangle their thoughts from their emotions.

Workbook Exercise

Try accurately reflecting on your own feelings or those of a friend. Write down a recent emotional experience and then summarize it as objectively as possible.

_____

_____

_____

_____

_____

Level Three: Reading a Person's Behavior

Some folks struggle to identify their own emotions due to past experiences or learned behavior. This is where you come in. Observe their emotional state and label or guess their feelings. It's okay to be wrong; only they know how they truly feel.

Workbook Exercise

Practice reading someone's behavior and guessing their emotions. It could be a friend, family member, or even a coworker. Write down your observations and guesses, and see how they respond when you validate their feelings.

_____

_____

_____

_____

_____

Level Four: Understanding the Person's History and Biology

Our past experiences and biology shape our emotional reactions. Understanding this can deepen your level of validation. For instance, if your friend had a traumatic experience with a dog, it makes sense that they might be uncomfortable around one.

Workbook Exercise

Reflect on your own emotional reactions in the context of your past experiences and biology. Write down a situation where your past influenced your feelings, and consider how understanding that can help you validate yourself.

_____
_____
_____
_____
_____

Level Five: Normalizing Emotional Reactions

Sometimes, just knowing that our emotions are normal can be incredibly reassuring. Emotionally sensitive individuals often feel like they're "too much," but realizing that anyone would feel a certain way in a given situation can be liberating.

Workbook Exercise

Identify a situation in which you or someone you know had an emotional reaction. Explain why this reaction is perfectly normal. Write down how this knowledge helps you or them feel validated.

Level Six: Radical Genuineness

At the highest level of validation, there's radical genuineness. This is when you deeply understand someone's emotions because you've experienced something similar. You're on the same emotional wavelength. Sharing your own experience as equals can strengthen relationships and enhance emotional management.

Workbook Exercise

Reflect on a time when you experienced radical genuineness from someone. How did it make you feel? How did it affect your connection with that person? How can you use this level of validation in your own relationships?

_____

_____

_____

_____

_____

Understanding and practicing these levels of validation can work wonders in your life and in the lives of those around you. Validation strengthens bonds and empowers us to manage our emotions effectively.

GIVE Skills

GIVE skills are like the Swiss Army knife of effective communication. They are especially handy when dealing with individuals who may be emotionally sensitive or challenging to connect with. Let's break them down one by one:

Gentle (Be)

Think of being gentle as having a soft touch in your interactions. Imagine you're holding a delicate butterfly in your hand—you wouldn't want to crush it, right? Similarly, be mindful of your tone, body language, and words. Avoid being harsh, judgmental, or confrontational. Instead, opt for kindness and patience.

Exercise: The Gentle Check-in

Take a moment to reflect on a recent interaction that might not have gone so well. Now, rewrite your response with a gentle tone and demeanor. What changes did you make? How does it feel different? Write your answers below.

_____

_____

_____

_____

_____

Interested (Act)

Showing genuine interest in others can work wonders in building rapport. When you actively engage with someone, it conveys that you value their thoughts and feelings. Be an attentive listener, ask open-ended questions, and show curiosity about their world.

Exercise: The Curiosity Challenge

Practice active listening with a friend or family member. Ask them about something you've never discussed before and genuinely listen to their response. How did their body language change? Did the conversation flow more smoothly? Share your observations below.

_____
_____
_____
_____

Validate (Mentioned Above)

Validation is like giving someone an emotional high-five. It's acknowledging their feelings without judgment. It doesn't mean you have to agree with everything they say, but you're letting them know their emotions are valid.

Exercise: The Validation Voyage

Think of a recent situation where someone shared their feelings with you. Write down how you validated their emotions. How did it make them feel? How did it make you feel? Share your insights below.

_____
_____
_____
_____

Easy Manner (Use An)

An easy manner is all about staying calm and composed, even in the face of chaos. Avoid getting defensive or aggressive. Instead, maintain your emotional balance and create a safe space for the other person to express themselves.

Exercise: The Zen Zone

Recall a time when you stayed calm in a difficult conversation. What techniques did you use to keep your cool? How did it affect the outcome? Share your strategies below.

_____
_____
_____
_____
_____

Did you know that research has shown that using GIVE skills can lead to improved relationships and decreased conflicts? It's true! A study found that individuals who underwent DBT training, including GIVE skills, experienced reduced anger and hostility in their relationships (Wu et al., 2023).

Morgan's Story

I'll tell you about how I used the GIVE skills with my friend Morgan when she called me to vent a few months ago. Morgan's voice sounded shaky and tired as she spilled her work problems to me- she was dealing with tons of tasks, coworkers making demands, and a boss who was always dissatisfied. You could feel the stress in Morgan's voice, and it seemed like tears were about to burst out.

My first impulse was to jump in with a bunch of solutions. I wanted to tell Morgan exactly what she should do to fix her work issues. After all, I really cared about Morgan and my first thought was that giving quick fixes would make everything better. But then I remembered the magic of GIVE skills.

Instead of bombarding Morgan with advice, I took a deep breath and reminded myself to be gentle, interested, validating, and keep things easygoing. So, I started by just listening carefully to Morgan's story. I didn't interrupt, and I gave her my complete attention. You could hear the relief in Morgan's voice when she realized that someone truly wanted to hear about her troubles.

As Morgan continued to pour her heart out, I knew it was time to validate her feelings. I told her, "Morgan, it sounds like you're going through a really tough time at work. It's totally understandable that you're feeling overwhelmed and frustrated. Anyone in your shoes would feel the same way." It was like a weight lifted from Morgan's voice when she heard those words.

Throughout our chat, I made sure to stay calm and relaxed, even though Morgan's emotions were running high. I didn't get upset along with her as she shared her problems with her colleagues and her boss. Instead, I focused on supporting Morgan by creating a safe space for her to let it all out.

By the time our conversation wrapped up, Morgan's tone had changed from despair to relief. She thanked me for being there and truly listening. Morgan admitted she'd been keeping her frustrations bottled up, worried that no one would understand. But thanks to the power of GIVE skills, she felt heard and supported.

In the following weeks, Morgan and I grew even closer. Our friendship deepened because Morgan knew that she could always come to me to express her feelings without judgment. She often says how grateful she was for our talk that day.

This story shows how using GIVE skills can transform not just individual conversations but also the dynamics of a friendship. By choosing kindness over advice, we build a stronger bond based on trust and understanding. Sometimes, the best way to support someone is to simply be a good listener, offer validation, and stay calm.

Remember, creating connections with others is all about compassion and understanding. These skills are not just tools; they're the building blocks of healthy relationships.

FAST Skills

Self-respect is the foundation of all healthy relationships, starting with the one you have with yourself. When you respect yourself, you're more likely to set boundaries, communicate effectively, and make decisions that align with your values.

FAST skills are all about maintaining self-respect while interacting with others, especially in situations where you might be tempted to give in or compromise too much. FAST is an acronym for: be **F**air, no **A**pologies, **S**tick to values, be **T**ruthful. Let's break down each component (Linehan, 2023).

Be Fair

Start by identifying a recent situation where you felt your self-respect was compromised. Write it down and describe what happened.

Now, ask the questions:

- Am I being fair to myself?
- Did I clearly express what I need and what I am feeling?
- Did I listen to the other person's perspective?

Workbook Exercise

Fill in the blanks below with your thoughts and feelings from the situation:

In this situation, I believe I was fair to myself by _____. However, I could have improved my fairness by _____. Next time, I will make sure to _____.

No Apologies

Think about a time when you apologized but you didn't need to. Write down the situation and what you apologized for.

Now, ask yourself:

- Why did I apologize?
- What were my true feelings in that moment?
- How could I have expressed my feelings without apologizing unnecessarily?

Workbook Exercise

Complete this sentence based on the situation you described:

In that situation, I apologized for _____. Looking back, I realize I didn't need to apologize because _____. Next time, I will express my feelings by _____.

Stick to Your Values

Take a moment to reflect on your core values. Write down the top three values that are important to you.

Now, ask yourself:

- Have I compromised my values in any recent interactions?
- How did it make me feel?
- What can I do to stick to my values while interacting with others?

Workbook Activity

Write down your top three values and brainstorm ways to uphold them in your daily interactions.

_____

_____

_____

_____

_____

_____

_____

_____

_____

Be Truthful

Think about a situation where you weren't entirely truthful. Write it down and describe why you chose not to be honest.

Now, ask yourself:

- What was my fear or motivation for not telling the truth?
- How would being truthful have improved the situation?
- What can I do to practice honesty in similar situations in the future?

Workbook Exercise

Reflect on the situation and complete this sentence:

In that situation, I was not entirely truthful because _____. In the future, I will be more honest by _____.

Studies have shown that incorporating FAST skills into your interactions can lead to improved self-esteem, healthier relationships, and reduced emotional distress (Flynn et al., 2019).

Many times throughout my young adult life, I found myself in situations where I felt pressured to agree to something my mom wanted me to do but that I didn't want to do. Instead of being truthful about my feelings, I apologized and gave in. It left me feeling resentful and like I had betrayed my own values. But after learning about FAST skills, I realized I could have handled the situation differently, sticking to my values and maintaining my self-respect.

Combining the Skills

My mother would constantly interrupt me during conversations, making it difficult for me to express my emotions or thoughts. Here's how I would combine DEAR MAN, GIVE, and FAST to address the issue:

1. **Describe:** Start by calmly describing the situation. "I've noticed that during our conversations, I often get interrupted when I'm trying to share my thoughts."
2. **Express:** Express your feelings and thoughts using 'I' statements. "I feel frustrated and unheard when this happens, and I believe it's essential for me to have a chance to speak."
3. **Assert:** Clearly state what you want or need. "I would appreciate it if you could let me finish speaking before responding."
4. **Reinforce:** Reinforce why your request is essential. "This will create a more respectful relationship for us."
5. **Mindful:** Stay focused on the issue at hand and avoid getting emotional or sidetracked.
6. **Appear Confident:** Maintain eye contact, use a calm tone, and practice good posture.
7. **Negotiate:** Be open to a discussion about how to improve communication between both of you.

Additionally, remember to be Gentle, Interested, Validate, and maintain an Easy Manner to foster a positive relationship. Be Fair in your request, avoid unnecessary Apologies, Stick to your Values, and always be Truthful to maintain your self-respect.

Let's add some extra context. Studies have shown that using a combination of DEAR MAN, GIVE, and FAST skills can significantly improve interpersonal effectiveness and reduce conflicts in various settings (May et al., 2016).

Combining DEAR MAN, GIVE, and FAST is a great tool to have for effective communication and maintaining healthy relationships. Practice these skills regularly and watch how they transform your interactions with others. I have left a space below for you to practice this skill. Take a moment and think of a situation where you want to find your voice, where you want to speak up. Jot down what you would say. Take your time and lean into the skills laid out above.

_____

_____

_____

_____

_____

In this chapter, we jumped into crucial skills and techniques that can revolutionize your relationships and communication style. Here's a quick recap:

- **Validation vs. Invalidation:** Marsha Linehan's six levels of validation are your guide to forming stronger connections with others. These levels include paying attention, reflecting back, understanding context and history, acknowledging validity, and treating people with respect. Validation is the superpower behind effective communication.
- **GIVE skills:** These four valuable skills are your tools for nurturing and preserving relationships. Try the GIVE exercise to apply these skills and see your connections thrive.

- **FAST skills (for self-respect):** As you navigate interpersonal effectiveness, safeguard your self-respect. The FAST exercise strengthens your self-respect and reinforces your convictions.
- **Combining DEAR MAN, GIVE, and FAST:** The real magic happens when you combine these skills. DEAR MAN empowers assertive communication, GIVE fosters positive relationships, and FAST preserves your self-respect. Together, they're your ticket to navigate even the trickiest interpersonal situations.

As you embark upon mastering these skills, remember that practice is key. Real-life situations will be your greatest teachers. Keep your goals clear, your words kind, and your self-respect intact. Also, forgive yourself for times when you slip up and don't use these skills. Just try again next time.

You now possess the tools to build stronger connections, gracefully resolve conflicts, and maintain your self-worth in any interaction. With DEAR MAN, GIVE, FAST, and the art of validation, you're on your way to becoming an interpersonal effectiveness expert.

Key Takeaways Week 8

- Understand the importance of validation in your interactions.
- Marsha Linehan's 6 levels of Validation:
  - Pay Attention: Give your full attention to the other person.
  - Reflect Back: Repeat or paraphrase what the other person has said to show you're listening.
  - Read Minds: Try to understand the other person's thoughts and feelings.

- Understand based on Personal Context/History: Consider the person's background and experiences.
- Acknowledge What's Valid: Recognize the legitimacy of the other person's emotions and perspective.
- Show Equality: Treat the other person with respect and as an equal.
- Explore ways to practice each type of validation to improve your relationships.
- Learn the GIVE skills for effective communication:
  - Be Gentle: Approach interactions with kindness and respect.
  - Act Interested: Show genuine interest in what the other person is saying.
  - Validate: Acknowledge the other person's feelings and experiences.
  - Use an Easy Manner: Keep the conversation light and relaxed.
- Self-respect is crucial in interpersonal interactions.
- FAST stands for:
  - Be Fair: Treat yourself and others with fairness and equity.
  - No Apologies: Avoid apologizing excessively or unnecessarily.
  - Stick to Your Values: Maintain your personal values and boundaries.
  - Be Truthful: Be honest and sincere in your interactions.
- Combine the DEAR MAN, GIVE, and FAST skills to create a comprehensive approach to effective communication and interpersonal effectiveness.
- By using these skills in synergy, you can navigate various situations and relationships with confidence and respect.

In the space between stimulus and response, there is a space. In that space is our power to choose our response. In our response lies our growth and our freedom.

— VIKTOR E. FRANKL

CONCLUSION

Continuing the Journey

We've journeyed together through the pages of this workbook, exploring the intricate and empowering terrain of DBT. As we come to the conclusion of this incredible expedition, it's a perfect time to pause and reflect on the profound insights we've gathered along the way.

Mindfulness: Our voyage through the world of mindfulness has shown us that it goes beyond merely being present in the moment; it's about immersing ourselves fully in the here and now, free from judgment. By embracing mindfulness, you've unlocked the power to enhance emotional regulation, discern judgmental thoughts, and make wiser, more intentional decisions in your life.

Wise Mind: The concept of finding the delicate balance between emotion mind and reasonable mind has been a guiding North star on our journey. Wise mind exercises have lit up the path, demonstrating that even in the face of life's most challenging situations, you can pause, breathe, and tap into your inner wisdom for guidance.

Distress Tolerance: Our discussions about distress tolerance have underscored the significance of not only managing but also surviving emotional distress. We've learned that acceptance is the crucial first step, and together, we've delved into a treasure trove of tools like TIP Skills, the STOP method, and the creation of a personalized Distress Tolerance Kit.

Radical Acceptance: We've embarked on the profound practice of embracing reality without judgment. We've seen how resistance to acceptance can be overcome through persistence and practice, paving the way for profound healing and unprecedented personal growth.

Emotions: Our expedition has brought us face-to-face with the profound truth that all emotions, without exception, are natural and valid. By learning to understand and work with your emotions, you've taken monumental steps toward achieving emotional well-being.

Problem-solving: We've equipped ourselves with a diverse toolkit for effective problem-solving, from the meticulous process of defining issues to the creative art of brainstorming solutions and the clarity of determining desired outcomes.

Interpersonal Effectiveness: Our exploration of interpersonal effectiveness has illuminated the importance of clarifying priorities and skillfully navigating the intricate web of human relationships. The DEAR MAN, GIVE, and FAST skills have been our trusted companions on this leg of the journey.

Combining Skills: Together, we've witnessed how these skills can harmonize and intertwine into a holistic approach to managing emotions, relationships, and life's multifaceted challenges.

As we conclude this expedition through the pages of this workbook, it's important to remember that the path to mastering these skills is not always linear. In fact, many people, myself included, find themselves embarking on the DBT path more than once. With each round, we deepen our understanding and proficiency, nurturing the flame of hope and fostering personal growth.

This workbook is not just a one-time guide: It's your map and compass for life's twists and turns. Whenever you need a refresher or a dose of motivation, know that you can return to these pages. If you have filled up the pages provided, feel free to grab a journal or any notebook and repeat the exercises there. Your experiences are valid, and your emotions matter profoundly. By applying these DBT skills, you're taking significant strides toward creating a more fulfilling and balanced life.

Before we part ways on this incredible expedition, I'd like to ask one last favor: if you've found this workbook helpful, please consider leaving a review. Your feedback will serve as a beacon, making it easier for others who may be seeking this resource to find it and embark on their own transformative journey of self-discovery and growth.

Thank you for being a part of this wonderful time. You hold within you the power to transform your life, one mindful step at a time. Embrace it, my friend, and never stop growing.

Warmest Regards,

Anna

Thank You

I really appreciate you buying and finishing this book. I'm SO THANKFUL for your support and hope this book has been beneficial to you.

There are numerous books on this subject, so I'm grateful and appreciative that you chose this one.

Before you go, I wanted to ask you for one last small favor. **It would be very helpful to me if you considered leaving a review on the platform. One of the best and simplest ways to support books from independent authors like me is to leave a review.**

Your opinions are very valuable to me. I'll be able to support other readers by continuing to write books like this. To hear from you would mean so much. I read every single review submitted.

REFERENCES

Ackerman, C. (2019, June 19). *Interpersonal effectiveness: 9 worksheets & examples*. Positive Psychology. https://positivepsychology.com/interpersonal-effectiveness/

A.J. (2023, August 21). *90 top quotes from radical acceptance*. Elevate Society. https://elevatesociety.com/quotes-from-radical-acceptance/#:~:text=%22May%20I%20love%20and%20accept

BetterHelp Editorial Team. (2018, January 23). *Mothers with borderline personality disorder: How to cope*. Better Help. https://www.betterhelp.com/advice/teenagers/mothers-with-borderline-personality-disorder-common-symptoms-and-treatment/

Chapman, A. L. (2006). Dialectical behavior therapy: Current indications and unique elements. *Psychiatry* (Edgmont), *3*(9), 62–68. https://www.ncbi.nlm.nih.gov/pmc/articles/PMC2963469/

Charlie Health Editorial Team. (2023, April 29). *ACCEPTS: A useful DBT skill for stress*. Charlie Health. https://www.charliehealth.com/post/accepts-dbt-skill#:~:text=An%20ACCEPTS%20DBT%20worksheet%20is

Cherry, K. (2019). *Psychology and life quotes from Carl Rogers*. Verywell Mind. https://www.verywellmind.com/carl-rogers-quotes-2795693

Compitus, K. (2020, October 1). *What are distress tolerance skills? Your ultimate DBT toolkit*. Positive Psychology. https://positivepsychology.com/distress-tolerance-skills/

Cuncic, A. (2021, May 26). *What is radical acceptance?* Verywell Mind. https://www.verywellmind.com/what-is-radical-acceptance-5120614

Do we even need them? Your guide to understanding emotions. (2017, November 7). Sunrise Residential Treatment Center. https://sunrisertc.com/emotions-list/

Emeritus, P. (2019). *Marsha Linehan* . Washington.edu. https://depts.washington.edu/uwbrtc/our-team/marsha-linehan/

Emotional regulation quotes-Miya Yamanouchi. (2023). Goodreads. https://www.goodreads.com/quotes/tag/emotional-regulation

Flynn, D., Joyce, M., Spillane, A., Wrigley, C., Corcoran, P., Hayes, A., Flynn, M., Wyse, D., Corkery, B., & Mooney, B. (2019). Does an adapted dialectical behaviour therapy skills training programme result in positive outcomes for participants with a dual diagnosis? A mixed methods study. *Addiction Science & Clinical Practice, 14*(1). https://doi.org/10.1186/s13722-019-0156-2

Hanh, T. N. (2023, August 18). *Inspiring quotes to live by: Embracing DBT skills for personal growth and transformation.* Grouport Therapy. https://www.grouporttherapy.com/blog/dialectical-behavior-therapy-quotes

Inspiring quotes to live by: Embracing DBT skills for personal growth and transformation. (2023, August 18). Grouport Therapy. https://www.grouporttherapy.com/blog/dialectical-behavior-therapy-quotes#:~:text=Mindfulness%20Quotes&text=%22The%20present%20moment%20is%20filled

Kabat-Zinn, J. (2019). *What is mindfulness?* Greater Good. https://greatergood.berkeley.edu/topic/mindfulness/definition

Lavender, J. M., Tull, M. T., DiLillo, D., Messman-Moore, T., & Gratz, K. L. (2016). Development and validation of a state-based measure of emotion dysregulation. *Assessment, 24*(2), 197–209. https://doi.org/10.1177/1073191115601218

Linehan, M. (n.d.). *Problem solving skill*. Dialectical Behavior Therapy (DBT) Tools. https://dbt.tools/distress_tolerance/problem-solving.php

Linehan, M. (2023a). *FAST skill*. Dialectical Behavior Therapy (DBT) Tools. https://dbt.tools/interpersonal_effectiveness/fast.php#:~:text=The%20FAST%20skill%20is%20an

Lo, I. (2023, August 8). *I have a mother with borderline personality disorder*. Medium. https://imilo.medium.com/i-have-a-mother-with-borderline-personality-disorder-107f15dc7ea3

Lorandini, J. (2019, April 16). *Opposite action for overwhelming emotions: How to make it work for you*. Suffolk DBT. https://suffolkdbtjl.com/opposite-action/#:~:text=What%20Is%20Opposite%20Action%3F

Main, P. (2022, December 2). *Carl Rogers' theory*. Structural Learning. https://www.structural-learning.com/post/carl-rogers-theory#:~:text=According%20to%20Carl%20Rogers

May, J. M., Richardi, T. M., & Barth, K. S. (2016). Dialectical behavior therapy as treatment for borderline personality disorder. *Mental Health Clinician*, 6(2), 62–67. https://doi.org/10.9740/mhc.2016.03.62

Parent with borderline personality disorder: Healing from your trauma. (2023, August 1). Eggshell Therapy and Coaching. https://eggshelltherapy.com/bpdparent/

Rowen, K. (2022, May 31). *Half-Smiling & willing hands*. DBT Center of Orange County. https://www.dbtcenteroc.com/half-smiling-willing-hands/

Tull, M. (2013, July 30). *Distress tolerance in post traumatic stress disorder*. Verywell Mind. https://www.verywellmind.com/distress-tolerance-2797294

6 life changing skills to successfully manage your next emotional crisis. (2017, September 13). Sunrise Residential Treatment Center. https://sunrisertc.com/distress-tolerance-skills/

Understanding the levels of validation. (2012, February 5). Psych Central. https://psychcentral.com/blog/emotionally-sensitive/2012/02/understanding-the-levels-of-validation#7

Using ABC please to manage overwhelming emotions with DBT. (2023, August 18). Grouport Therapy. https://www.grouporttherapy.com/blog/abc-please-dbt#:~:text=ABC%20PLEASE%20is%20an%20acronym

Vaughan, S. (2023, September 18). *DBT distress tolerance skills: Tip skill, stop skill, and more.* Psychotherapy Academy. https://psychotherapyacademy.org/section/distress-tolerance-skills/

What skills: Observe, describe, participate. (2023, September 28). DBT Self Help. https://dbtselfhelp.com/dbt-skills-list/mindfulness/what-skills/

Wu, S.-I., Liu, S.-I., Wu, Y.-J., Huang, L.-L., Liu, T., Kao, K.-L., & Lee, Y.-H. (2023). The efficacy of applying the interpersonal effectiveness skills of dialectical behavior therapy into communication skills workshop for clinical nurses. *Heliyon, 9*(3), e14066. https://doi.org/10.1016/j.heliyon.2023.e14066

Printed in Great Britain
by Amazon